W9-DCC-804

WITHDRAWN

RICHARD SCHLATTER, GENERAL EDITOR

Humanistic Scholarship in America
◄§ THE PRINCETON STUDIES §►

THE COUNCIL OF THE HUMANITIES
WHITNEY J. OATES, CHAIRMAN
PRINCETON UNIVERSITY

ANTHROPOLOGY

Eric R. Wolf

ART AND ARCHAEOLOGY

James S. Ackerman   Rhys Carpenter

CHINESE PAINTING

Wen Fong

CLASSICS

Eric A. Havelock

ENGLISH LITERATURE

David Daiches

FOREIGN LITERATURE

Henri Peyre

HISTORY

John Higham
Leonard Krieger   Felix Gilbert

LINGUISTICS

Eric P. Hamp   Karl D. Uitti
Rulon Wells

Their Authors

MODERN AMERICAN CRITICISM
Walter Sutton

MUSICOLOGY
Frank Ll. Harrison   Mantle Hood
Claude V. Palisca

THE ORIGINS OF AMERICAN
HUMANISTIC SCHOLARS
Robert H. Knapp

PHILOSOPHY
Roderick M. Chisholm   Herbert Feigl
William K. Frankena   John Passmore
Manley Thompson

RELIGION
Paul Ramsey, ed.
Philip H. Ashby   Robert M. Grant
James M. Gustafson   J. H. Nichols
Harry M. Orlinsky   John E. Smith
Claude Welch

RELIGION, A HUMANISTIC FIELD
Clyde A. Holbrook

The aim of these volumes is to present a critical account of American humanistic scholarship in recent decades. They have been commissioned by the Council of the Humanities, Whitney J. Oates, Chairman, of Princeton University and were made possible by a grant from the Ford Foundation.

—Richard Schlatter, General Editor.

The ORIGINS of AMERICAN HUMANISTIC SCHOLARS

ROBERT H. KNAPP

PROFESSOR OF PSYCHOLOGY
WESLEYAN UNIVERSITY

PRENTICE-HALL, INC.   ENGLEWOOD CLIFFS   NEW JERSEY

CARL A. RUDISILL LIBRARY
LENOIR RHYNE COLLEGE

378
K 72 o

© 1964 by the Trustees of Princeton University. Copyright 1964 under International and Pan-American Copyright Conventions. All rights reserved. No part of this book may be reproduced in any form, by mimeograph or other means, without permission in writing from Prentice-Hall, Inc., Englewood Cliffs, New Jersey. Manufactured in the United States of America. Library of Congress Catalog Card Number: 64-16031

C-64260

PRENTICE-HALL INTERNATIONAL, INC., LONDON
PRENTICE-HALL OF AUSTRALIA, PTY., LTD., SYDNEY
PRENTICE-HALL OF CANADA, LTD., TORONTO
PRENTICE-HALL OF INDIA (PRIVATE) LTD., NEW DELHI
PRENTICE-HALL OF JAPAN, INC., TOKYO
PRENTICE-HALL DE MEXICO, S.A., MEXICO CITY

50,307
July, 1965

ᙓᔕ To my mother ᔤᕀ
Helene D. Knapp

FOREWORD

What is the purpose of humanistic scholarship? What in fact does the humanist scholar do? The Ford Humanities Project under the direction of the Council of the Humanities at Princeton University has been looking at American humanistic scholarship of recent decades, trying to answer these questions and trying to describe that scholarship, attempting to sift the imaginative, the original, and the admirable from the pedantic, the conventional, and the superficial.

We have commissioned about a dozen volumes by recognized scholars in various fields. These volumes will give us an account of American humanistic scholarship, enabling us to see just what that scholarship has contributed to the culture of America and the world. From the outset, the Ford Humanities Project decided that it would be wise to have some non-American critics looking at American humanistic scholarship and, in addition, if we could find the right person, a nonhumanistic critic as well. We cannot call Professor Knapp a "nonhumanist" merely because he is a psychologist; but he is a social scientist by profession and he was the obvious person for us to choose since he had already made such discerning studies of American men of science.

The facts he has assembled in this essay and the comments he makes will be of concern to all humanists. He shows clearly that one serious shortcoming of humanistic scholarship is its provincialism, its regionalism and the narrowness of its social base. Too large a percentage of humanistic scholars are recruited from a relatively small number of undergraduate colleges, most of them relatively high-cost private institutions located in the northeast part of the country. The graduates of these schools who go on to become professional scholars in the humanities get their doctorates in too small a number of graduate schools, either private universities in the East or a few outstanding state universities in the West. And it is in these institutions of course that the matured scholars eventually settle. In comparison, the sciences are able to recruit from a much wider geographical, institutional, and social base. Every state in the union is training undergraduate science majors and doctors in sciences, and mature scientists are at work in laboratories in a great variety of institutions located in every part of the United States. To put this another way, relatively few American universities and colleges provide as hospitable a climate for the study of the humanities as they do for the sciences and these few recruit their students from a relatively narrow geographic and social base compared to the sciences. The charge that the humanities are still in pragmatic America an avocation of the rich and genteel is not true—but most of us who call ourselves humanists wax more indignant at the charge than we would if it were entirely baseless. Professor Knapp's statistics show us why. We must try then to spread humanistic scholarship more widely in our colleges and universities.

Professor Knapp has many other interesting things to say. He points out again that the humanities must have more financial support if we are to overcome the present imbalance in our culture. He has, incidently, very flattering things to say about historical studies—which, of course, cannot fail to please the editor who thinks of himself as a historian.

RICHARD SCHLATTER
General Editor

PREFACE

The purpose of this volume is to explore the academic origins, and to some extent the attitudes, of the fraternity of American scholars devoted to the advancement of the humanities. It is my hope that this book, especially in conjunction with other studies commissioned by the Council of the Humanities at Princeton, may provide some guidelines for educational policy and development affecting these areas. Unlike the other studies commissioned by the Council, this one has been prepared by a social scientist, is heavily statistical in character, and does not presume to judge the condition of the humanistic disciplines themselves.

In the final sense, this is a study in ecology—devoted to the question of the conditions under which a particular form of life will best thrive and prosper and those under which it will be blighted or perish. Few biologists would recognize it as such, for it deals with a very special form of life, the American humanistic scholar, and a very special type of environment, the collegiate and university institutions in which he thrives or languishes. But ecology it is and indeed it parallels similar studies devoted to the backgrounds of other varieties of eminent scholars or leaders.

At a time in history when *the two cultures* has become a tediously common phrase throughout academia it might be thought that the conflict of the sciences and the humanities would provide a focus in this book, particularly since I have written about scientists in *The Origins of American Scientists* (1953). But it does so only incidentally. Except in the final chapter, I have avoided entering into the tortuous question of the difference between the metaphysics of the two worlds, concerning which there is an increasingly vast literature, devoid of common terminology, shot through with ethical and moralistic preconceptions, and amazingly diverse in origins. A problem doubtless exists here, but I have, in part out of a sense of incompetence and in part out of impatience, avoided it. I have not altogether ignored, however, the relation of the humanities to other disciplines, including those of science, especially as it bears on the central problem of their cultural and educa-

xi

tional ecology. Indeed, the ratio relating the production of scientists to the production of humanistic scholars has proved most important in revealing the intellectual climate of an institution.

Just as I have bypassed the literature relating the humanities to the sciences and other disciplines, so to a large extent I have not pursued bibliographic research, chiefly because, apart from a half-dozen recent empirical studies alluded to, there is little of importance in the field, but also because the time devoted to this research appeared better assigned to other efforts. This neglect of careful and exhaustive bibliographic report is regrettable but may be excused on the grounds that empirical studies of the careers of American humanists have been fragmentary, obscure, and quickly outdated by the march of educational conditions and practice.

The general outline of the book falls into six main sections. The first chapter seeks to find either in history or in empirical statistics a tentative answer to the question of what constitute the humanities. The next five chapters are devoted to an examination of the baccalaureate origins of humanistic scholars in the United States over the past several decades. There follow two chapters devoted to graduate production in the humanities and the career patterns of recent Ph.D.'s in this area. The four succeeding chapters are devoted to the description of eight selected major universities that I visited in the spring of 1961 in an effort to understand the institutional and environmental factors shaping the quantity and quality of their production of humanistic scholars. In the last chapter, I discuss my impressions of the special intellectual postures characteristic of humanists—in comparison with those of scientists and other scholars known to me through earlier studies. It will be discerned, from the general scheme set forth above, that the problem of the academic ecology of the American humanist has been approached through multiple channels of evidence. With peculiar regularity the same answers have recurred. I have not therefore been confronted with the task of reconciling uncertain or paradoxical results, but rather with reporting a high degree of congruence from several sources of evidence.

I cannot forbear, before making acknowledgment of indebtedness to my several aides and benefactors, recounting an episode that stood at the very inception of the project. I mentioned to a humanistic colleague my intention to undertake this modest study. He ruefully remarked that I was indeed on the wrong track, that in fact I was pursuing "not the English bards but the Scotch reviewers." I had best, he admonished me, devote myself not to the humanistic scholar but to the creative artist. That his point had some merit is beyond dispute. Especially in literature and the arts, the eminent of academia are rarely distinguished practitioners, nor should this be expected of them, in view of their primary function as critics and teachers. Among historians and philosophers, however, the creators and the critics are alike members of academia, and the single individual commonly incorporates excellence in both departments. But in recognition of my friend's admonition, I have preferred throughout this study not the simple term *humanist* but rather the term *humanistic scholar*.

In a work of this character, one must mention the names of institutions, and occasionally the names of particular persons. I have sought to minimize such references so far as possible, especially the designation of particular persons in various university departments. My reasons are that the brevity of my visits and the complexities of a humanities department in a major university preclude the formation of any secure judgment of merit or responsibility. With respect to institutions, I have described eight of them individually, but here again I would like to interpose a caution. In previous published work, institutions have seized upon the various reported numerical indices either as grounds for indignation or as a basis for advertising their merit. I consider this regrettable and hope the publication of a few modest figures in this volume will not lead to similar consequences. One cannot, of course, always confidently equate quantity and quality. In any case, the rate or the number of the humanistic scholars emerging from an institution is attributable to many factors, primary among which is the quality and motivation of the students initially attracted. I would like then explicitly to disavow that these figures reflect merely the pedagogical effectiveness of the faculty or curriculum.

Some acknowledgment to those who contributed to this volume is surely now in order. Foremost, of course, is the Council of the Humanities at Princeton University, which provided the basic financing under a grant from the Ford Foundation. This study is one of a number under its sponsorship devoted to an examination of the humanistic disciplines in America. In the most primary sense, I am indebted to the National Academy of Sciences and its roster of doctorates granted from 1936 to the present. This remarkable compilation has made possible the assembling and manipulation of data that would be virtually unthinkable under other conditions. During the course of this inquiry I have had the assistance of a number of persons as statistical and clerical aides. Foremost of these is Mrs. Helen Ehlinger, and second only to her is Miss Linda Ehlinger, to whom I am indebted for many of the statistical analyses. Mrs. Ona Langer and Mrs. Beatrice Burford have ably assisted in preparing drafts of the manuscript. Grateful mention should also be made of Mrs. Matilda Welter who has undertaken a critical review of the text. Beyond these I am indebted to a number of my students who from time to time have engaged in various compilations and analyses of statistical information. Finally, I wish to acknowledge my special and grateful indebtedness to Martin Nemirow of Prentice-Hall, Inc., who has been of very great value in preserving me from obscurities of statistical expression and in providing a detailed and judicious review and editing of the entire text.

ROBERT H. KNAPP

CONTENTS

INTRODUCTION

This is a study of the American humanistic scholar, his origins, place of training, and, in some degree, his intellectual outlook. At the outset it should be recognized that the humanistic disciplines have a comparatively ancient and much honored history in the European intellectual tradition with which the American humanist has and does claim strong allegiance. Probably more than in the sciences and technologies, American humanism remains allied to European scholarly patterns. Indeed, much humanistic scholarship in contemporary America deals essentially with European materials, especially in literature and the arts.

The movement of the humanities from the European to the American scene was initially accomplished without, for the most part, changing the European tradition of humanistic study; until comparatively late within the American system, *humanities* designated the study of classical languages *per se*. Gradually, following the Civil War, the term began to take on in this country an extended meaning. The humanities came to include the study of "vernacular" and contemporary literature, modern philosophy, and very recently the fine arts. Indeed, the core of the humanities as they were originally conceived, the study of Latin, Greek, and possibly Hebrew literature, gave way in importance to these new inclusions. Still, the classical languages requirement in the name of humanism persisted to a surprisingly late date among eastern private universities. At Princeton and Yale, Latin or Greek was still a prerequisite for admission in the 1930's.

The structure of contemporary American colleges and universities commonly reveals a recognized division of academic disciplines that are "functionally" identified as the humanities. These humanistic fields have felt a shared common interest resting upon several circumstances. One is a common opposition to the forces represented by the technological and utilitarian educational aims. In good part, too, the grouping has been a product of bureaucratic and administrative convenience. But beyond these considerations, and with qualifications, I believe the humanities are bound together by certain final attitudes toward the intellectual enterprise; not, as in the sciences, a clearly defined preference for experiment and methodology, but rather a common respect for style, taste, and sagacity as educational aims.

A decade ago, I surveyed the emergence of the American scientific profession[1] and reported on the historical evolution of the natural sciences in a number of liberal arts colleges. I described the shifts in curricular emphasis and the ensuing changes in production of scientists and other scholars from private colleges. Almost all private colleges began with a strong sectarian commitment and with particular concern for religious training. Here the humanities played a leading ancillary role. Conspicuously absent was any serious concern with the sciences, technologies, or utilitarian education. This condition persisted until the Civil War. Then, first in the more liberal eastern colleges and presently elsewhere, there occurred what I designated the "first secularization." In this period in which "natural philosophy" characteristically gave way to the establishment of the sciences and technologies, there was a strong pragmatic and utilitarian flavor. This was the period in which the Ph.D., mainly of German precedent, first took root in our system of higher education; at that time the Ph.D. was largely limited to the sciences. Meanwhile conflicts between the "classicists" and the sciences flared up with predictable regularity. At varying dates between the Civil War and World War II, the curricular structure and institutional dedication of these colleges shifted from the humanities to the sciences and technologies.

But this proved to be an impermanent state of affairs, for many colleges then underwent a "second secularization," in which there was a return to a liberal tradition and at least a partial recovery of the status and dignity accorded the humanities. Now, however, the humanities lacked their prior alliance with religious concerns. This "second secularization" proved most marked among eastern colleges whose humanistic tradition had been most deeply ingrained and who had proved most effective in resisting or mollifying the "first secularization." Among these eastern colleges the humanities in our time have shown an unusual vigor while the sciences, despite abundant subsidy, fail to make comparable claim upon the interests of students.

Although this pattern was observed in private liberal arts colleges, I believe it characterized the course followed by our major Ivy League universities as well. With perhaps one exception, the University of

[1] Robert H. Knapp and H. B. Goodrich, *The Origins of American Scientists* (U. of Chicago, 1953).

Pennsylvania, these universities also began as sectarian institutions powerfully fusing religious and humanistic commitments. Most, if not all, showed some clear concessions to the rise of American science and technology in the Victorian period. As examples, one may look at the establishment of the sciences at Harvard, and the Sheffield School at Yale. Yet in spite of such additions, the "first secularization" did not "take" in the Ivy League universities. Science and technology were never able to establish themselves as the regnant forces behind the intellectual life of these institutions. As we shall see, these institutions remain the bastions of humanistic scholarship whether we consider the scholarly careers of their graduates, the ratio of doctorates granted in the sciences and humanities, or the character of those who exercise leadership within them, or yet other lines of evidence.

Within the great system of public universities, particularly those rooted in the frontier areas of the nineteenth century, the story, with very few exceptions, is entirely different. The American public university was largely a product of frontier democracy, just as the private universities of the East represented an earlier principle of exclusiveness and even aristocracy. The Civil War period saw great impetus given to the further development of these state systems of higher education through the passing of the Morrill Land Grant Act, which provided for the foundation and maintenance of colleges "where the leading object shall be to teach such branches of learning as are related to agriculture and the mechanical arts . . . in order to promote the liberal and practical education of the industrial classes." The spirit of the Morrill Act, reflecting the spirit of the "first secularization" was explicit in its emphasis upon essentially utilitarian and pragmatic values, specifically technologies, though with some apparent reluctance the act states that the "humanities shall not be neglected." Of course, not all state institutions should be identified with the act. Ohio State, for example, is strictly a land grant institution, but Wisconsin and Berkeley represent a combination of an earlier established state institution with a land grant addition; Indiana University, on the other hand, has never been subject to land grant benefits. Still, the Morrill Act defines an educational philosophy that to greater or lesser degree conditioned the entire public university system and gave a great democratic and utilitarian thrust to education in our then frontier regions.

In this climate, the humanities found themselves unhonored in comparison with their position in the great private universities of the East.

Only among the best and only by force of great numbers of schools and enrolled students do the state universities compare in the humanities with the more ancient and established private universities of the East. In the sciences and the technologies, on the other hand, the position of the state university is clearly ascendant. Thus, in simple summary, the humanities were at best superimposed upon the grass-roots pragmatism of the state university system, while among the eastern private colleges and universities the humanities constituted the strong traditional core, against which the sciences and technologies claimed but limited historical victories. That some sort of convergence of educational style is now in process in both types of universities is doubtless true. But these historical differences remain still in striking evidence.

In subsequent chapters of this book there will be frequent occasion to speak of the humanities collectively and to report statistics in which the several humanistic fields under consideration are combined. Some case then should be made at this juncture for the "unity of the humanities," lest it be assumed that fields that move in quite independent paths and do not share a common destiny in the intellectual life of our nation have been lumped together capriciously and without justification. Two cases, it seems to me, can be made for the effective unity of the fields we have designated "the humanities," namely history, English, foreign languages, philosophy, and the fine arts. The first is intuitive and a priori, the second empirical. Let us consider the intuitive arguments first.

The first intuitive argument rests in the common history of the humanistic disciplines. The studies of literature, history, the arts, languages, and philosophy have tended to proceed from the same European models, to find their reception in the same institutions and during the same periods on the American scene, and to share a common administrative grouping in most cases. Thus, there is a strong presumption that they possess some final like-mindedness.

Second, the humanities almost without exception are primarily concerned with some aspect of the "human predicament"—the relation of man to man or man to his world. An astute critic could find exceptions to this assertion; still, in the main, the centrality of the human figure is clear in most humanistic disciplines.

Third, it appears that the humanities are bound together by a common concern with style and taste of expression, an apparent conviction that it is as important to speak well as to speak truthfully. The humanities tend to be verbal disciplines, not quantitative disciplines like the sciences.

Fourth, it appears that the humanities, as already suggested, tend to be more preoccupied with the human heritage than with the human future; at least this proposition has been forcefully advanced by at least two notable humanists, Howard Mumford Jones and Henri Peyre. In any event, the humanistic disciplines do not seem so concerned with control and prediction as do the physical sciences and perhaps even the social sciences.

These then are four grounds for asserting, intuitively, community of these fields. L. A. Ehlinger and I have, however, undertaken a second, empirical, approach to this question, by employing a statistical procedure known as factor analysis. The mathematical results of this process have been published elsewhere[2]; it will suffice here to review the general logic of this method and to indicate the relevance of our findings to the grouping of the humanistic disciplines. A factor analysis is essentially a mathematical device by which patterns of intercorrelations may be employed to identify groupings, clusters, or "families" that share traits in common. It has great advantages over the procedures of common human observation by which things are normally placed in categories since the method produces a mathematical statement of the number of "families" involved as well as the degree to which any particular item may be assigned to each "family."

We began by examining the record of doctorates granted by the thirty largest universities in the nation published by the National Academy of Sciences.[3] Next, we reduced to percentages the proportions granted in all major scholarly fields. At this juncture we determined the degree that each field was positively or negatively affiliated with every other. We posed the question, for example, "Is there a tendency among the thirty universities for a high percentage of doctorates in history to be accompanied by a high, intermediate, or low percentage in English or some other field?" The answers to such questions of cor-

[2] Robert H. Knapp and L. A. Ehlinger, "Styles of Scholarly Production" and "A Factorial Analysis of Fields of Scholarly Production," *Journal of Educational Research*, LVI, 5 and 9 (1963), 243-49 and 284-87.
[3] National Academy of Sciences, National Research Council, *Doctorate Production in United States Universities 1936-1956*, Publication #582. This publication is frequently and informally mentioned in the following chapters.

relation reflect the degree to which disciplines are positively or negatively associated with each other within the thirty universities. The resulting table of "correlations" enabled us to perform the next step, a factor analysis of academic fields.

The results of our factor analysis yielded three fairly distinctive families of academic disciplines. The first of these constituted all the recognized physical sciences; the second, the biological sciences. It is the third family of disciplines that concerns us here, the foremost nine of which are listed in Table I in order of their membership in this

TABLE I.

History	+ 82
Foreign languages	+ 79
English	+ 72
Sociology	+ 64
Philosophy	+ 58
Political science	+ 57
Anthropology	+ 45
Economics	+ 45
Fine arts and music	+ 21

grouping. Included here also is the "factor loading" for each of these disciplines, a number indicating by its magnitude the degree to which the field may be identified with this family. The first three are respectively history, foreign languages, and English, while the fifth is philosophy. Fine arts and music, a very small field numerically, occupies ninth position, and interspersed between these humanistic areas are some of the traditional social sciences. It is clear that this "family" is primarily composed of the humanities, secondarily of some of the social sciences. The top three representatives are the most important and numerous of the humanistic disciplines, while nowhere here do we find any of the biological or physical sciences.

This line of evidence therefore indicates that the humanistic fields considered here—namely, history, English, foreign languages, philosophy, and the fine arts and music—do indeed seem to share empirically a common fate within the major American universities. Where one thrives, others appear to thrive; when one languishes, others appear to lose force and suffer similarly. This finding suggests that there may be institutional factors of transcendant significance that make for a hos-

6

pitality or inhospitality to the humanities in general. It is toward an identification of these factors that a major part of this study is devoted.

I shall leave this problem for the present without more exhaustive examination. The ensuing chapters will, I believe, present detailed and abundant evidence that the humanities for many reasons do constitute a coherent and functionally unified body of disciplines.

❧ 2 ❧

A TYPOLOGY OF AMERICAN
COLLEGES AND UNIVERSITIES

The last decade has seen an almost obsessive concern among college administrators and professors with the classification and evaluation of American institutions of higher education. This has been actuated by the desire to compare achievements and to plot new courses of institutional development. Such concerns have inevitably raised the question of types and varieties of American higher educational institutions. In an earlier work[1] I have classified such institutions as public and private, universities and colleges, church-controlled and nondenominational, and by region, cost, and size, upon the a priori assumption that these represent meaningful categories. I shall seek here to approach the problem of classifying institutions in a quite different manner, that is, in terms of the type of scholar produced by each. This typology rests not upon a priori categories but rather upon statistical evidence from which an inductive classification is derived.

The preceding chapter was concerned only with the data obtained on doctoral production in the thirty largest graduate schools of the nation from 1936 to 1956. In the 1958 report of the National Academy of Sciences, however, there are data concerning the baccalaureate origins of all students who have taken doctorates during this period. This suggested that some form of statistical analysis might be undertaken employing this second body of information. It would permit determination of whether any type or class of institution appeared to be notably productive of, and hospitable toward, the humanities, as evidenced by a larger proportion of their graduates continuing to the doctorate in the humanistic disciplines as compared with other areas.

The National Academy of Sciences selected the ninety-five institutions yielding the greatest number of graduates who have subsequently taken a Ph.D. within the period from 1936 to 1956. For each of these ninety-five institutions the number of Ph.D.'s taking their bac-

---

[1] Robert H. Knapp and Joseph J. Greenbaum, *The Younger American Scholar: His Collegiate Origins* (U. of Chicago, 1953).

calaureate degrees from each of thirty-one fields of scholarship is recorded. In the development of the present study these numbers were combined under five main headings: physical sciences, biological sciences, humanities, social sciences, and education. It should also be noted that I took the liberty of eliminating certain categories and combining others. Thus, for example, history was classified among the humanities, while business and commerce were eliminated from this category. Next, for each institution the percentage of total baccalaureates who had taken doctorates in each of our five major categories was calculated. The resulting table of percentages for each institution yielded profiles that revealed immediately the areas of relative strength and weakness in scholarly production at any institutions. It should be emphasized here that this mode of analysis ignores the absolute number, and also ignores the ratio of scholars to graduates. It deals only with relative achievement in different areas of scholarship.

The statistical procedure employed here directly paralleled that used in the consideration of scholarly fields in the preceding chapter. But in this case correlations between each institution and every other were established, thus obtaining a measure of the degree to which their proportional scholarly output was similar or disparate. This 95-by-95 table of correlations was then subjected to a standard factor

TABLE 2. Loadings on 4 factors for 95
selected institutions.

Institution	Factor I Ivy League	Factor II Land Grant	Factor III Metropolitan- Teacher	Factor IV Technological
California (Berkeley)[a]	+ .44	+ .73	− .01	+ .52
CCNY	+ .43	+ .16	+ .52	+ .72
Illinois	+ .36	+ .54	+ .09	+ .76
Chicago	+ .84	+ .25	+ .17	+ .46
Wisconsin	+ .31	+ .93	+ .05	+ .20
Harvard	+ .90	− .08	− .01	+ .44
Minnesota	+ .35	+ .87	+ .12	+ .34
Columbia	+ .03	− .48	+ .69	+ .53
Michigan	+ .61	+ .36	+ .12	+ .70
NYU	+ .01	− .05	+ .94	+ .34
Cornell	+ .26	+ .86	− .16	+ .41

[a] For the sake of simplicity, abbreviated forms of the names of colleges and universities have been used in the tables. For full names, see the appendix on page 167.

TABLE 2.

Institution	Factor I Ivy League	Factor II Land Grant	Factor III Metropolitan- Teacher	Factor IV Technological
Ohio State	+ .25	+ .78	+ .28	+ .50
UCLA	+ .82	+ .24	+ .46	+ .26
Yale	+ .84	− .13	− .01	+ .54
Washington	+ .52	+ .47	+ .26	+ .67
Brooklyn	+ .71	+ .29	+ .33	+ .56
Penn State	+ .17	+ .79	+ .12	+ .58
MIT	+ .29	+ .20	+ .06	+ .94
Texas	+ .75	+ .12	+ .19	+ .63
Pennsylvania	+ .60	+ .02	+ .09	+ .80
Stanford	+ .79	+ .14	+ .44	+ .41
Northwestern	+ .79	+ .06	+ .30	+ .53
State U. of Iowa	+ .90	+ .24	+ .34	− .11
Purdue	+ .32	+ .61	+ .03	+ .73
Oberlin	+ .67	− .15	− .02	+ .73
Princeton	+ .75	− .29	− .16	+ .57
Iowa U.	+ .13	+ .87	− .11	+ .47
Nebraska	+ .10	+ .99	+ .12	− .06
Catholic U.	+ .25	− .86	− .41	− .21
Missouri	− .01	+ .93	+ .37	+ .07
Pittsburgh	+ .38	+ .33	+ .82	+ .30
Rutgers	− .05	+ .95	− .12	+ .29
Indiana	+ .45	+ .32	+ .57	+ .61
Utah	+ .45	+ .44	+ .22	+ .75
Syracuse	+ .41	+ .59	+ .69	+ .09
Kansas	+ .54	+ .59	+ .21	+ .56
Michigan State	− .06	+ .97	− .24	− .07
Cal Tech	+ .28	+ .23	+ .03	+ .93
Johns Hopkins	+ .38	+ .24	+ .06	+ .89
Dartmouth	+ .95	− .04	− .01	+ .32
North Carolina	+ .91	− .13	− .05	+ .41
Colorado U.	+ .61	+ .35	+ .13	+ .70
Utah State	+ .03	+ .96	+ .01	− .30
DePauw	+ .51	+ .57	+ .14	+ .63
Rochester	+ .46	+ .17	− .10	+ .87
Brown	+ .61	+ .24	− .02	+ .75
Carnegie Tech	+ .24	+ .12	+ .11	+ .96
Brigham Young	− .25	+ .95	00	− .17
Washington U.	+ .76	+ .23	+ .11	+ .60
Wayne State	+ .48	00	+ .70	+ .54
Florida	+ .23	+ .87	+ .26	+ .36
Boston U.	− .15	− .52	+ .73	− .41
Temple	+ .31	+ .13	+ .85	+ .42

TABLE 2.

Institution	Factor I Ivy League	Factor II Land Grant	Factor III Metropolitan- Teacher	Factor IV Technological
Swarthmore	+ .89	+ .17	+ .05	+ .43
Oklahoma	+ .45	+ .22	+ .47	+ .73
USC	+ .38	+ .02	+ .75	− .52
Kentucky	+ .31	+ .83	+ .11	+ .45
Kansas State	+ .06	+ .99	− .14	+ .08
Hunter	− .06	− .40	+ .35	− .85
Maryland	+ .03	+ .94	− .20	+ .30
Massachusetts	− .12	+ .91	− .37	− .13
LSU	+ .13	+ .91	00	+ .41
Miami (Ohio)	+ .78	+ .47	+ .09	+ .40
George Washington	+ .66	+ .74	+ .08	+ .11
Virginia	+ .82	− .11	− .12	+ .56
Western Reserve	+ .94	+ .30	+ .09	+ .06
Cincinnati	+ .45	+ .04	+ .28	+ .85
Washington State	− .05	+ .98	− .09	+ .19
Oregon State	− .11	+ .89	− .04	+ .45
West Virginia	+ .10	+ .79	+ .09	+ .60
Amherst	+ .91	− .38	− .02	+ .15
Oklahoma State	− .29	+ .93	− .09	− .20
Fordham	+ .98	+ .13	+ .14	+ .08
Notre Dame	+ .43	+ .08	+ .03	+ .90
Buffalo	+ .33	+ .27	+ .37	+ .83
Duke	+ .84	+ .08	+ .34	+ .43
Denver	+ .11	− .02	+ .95	− .25
Alabama	+ .36	− .27	+ .89	+ .07
RPI	+ .26	+ .19	+ .07	+ .95
Wesleyan	+ .89	− .23	− .15	+ .37
Reed	+ .71	+ .16	+ .19	+ .66
Emory	+ .61	+ .14	− .27	+ .74
St. Louis	+ .94	− .24	+ .04	+ .24
Wooster	+ .61	+ .02	+ .03	+ .80
Ohio	+ .24	+ .27	+ .86	+ .36
New Hampshire	+ .09	+ .80	+ .04	+ .59
North Texas	− .56	− .04	+ .79	+ .16
Oregon	− .09	− .48	+ .85	− .19
State C. of Iowa	− .46	− .18	+ .84	− .20
Tennessee	+ .02	+ .93	+ .20	+ .31
Idaho	− .14	+ .97	− .15	+ .09
Texas A. & M.	+ .10	+ .89	− .12	+ .43
Georgia	− .11	+ .99	00	− .11
Connecticut	+ .09	+ .96	− .10	− .23
Arkansas	+ .44	+ .77	+ .33	+ .33

analysis yielding four distinct factors.[2] These factors may be thought of as "modal patterns" of scholarly production to which each particular institution may be referred. Table 2 lists the ninety-five institutions, together with their loading on each of the four factors. These loadings express the degree to which a particular institution is positively or negatively identified with the "modal pattern" represented by each factor. It should be observed that the factor loadings ascribed to each institution are based entirely upon the pattern of their scholarly output, without preconceptions. Thus, no account is taken of the character of the student body, type of administration, traditions, or other such considerations. Bearing this in mind, let us examine the institutions that show a particular identification with each of our four factors to determine if any of these represents a type distinctively hospitable to the humanities.

For the four—as yet unlabeled—factors, I selected the institutions with very high loadings in each, that is to say, institutions most representative of factor 1, institutions most representative of factor 2, and two other similar groups for factor 3 and factor 4. For each of these four selected factor groups I calculated the percentage of each group's total Ph.D. production devoted to the humanities and the other four fields of scholarship. Figure 1 shows the average profile of each of the four factorial groups of institutions. I present here for graphic convenience the ratio of the mean percentage for each group to the mean percentage of all groups.

The first group of institutions is in fact notably high in the humanities, strong in the social sciences, moderately productive in the physical and biological sciences, but conspicuously low in the field of education. The institutions reported in Table 3 had factor loadings on the first factor exceeding +.80. It will be observed that in this group Ivy League institutions heavily predominate and that only three of the fifteen, the University of California, Los Angeles, the State University of Iowa, and the University of North Carolina, are publicly supported. It seems warranted to describe this factor as "Ivy League."

The second factor shows a contribution that is very heavy in the field of biological sciences, modest in the field of education, and low in the humanities. The twenty-three institutions listed in Table 4 yielded

[2] For detail on mathematical procedures involved, see Robert H. Knapp and L. A. Ehlinger, "Styles of Scholarly Production," *Journal of Educational Research,* LVI. 5 (1963), 243-49.

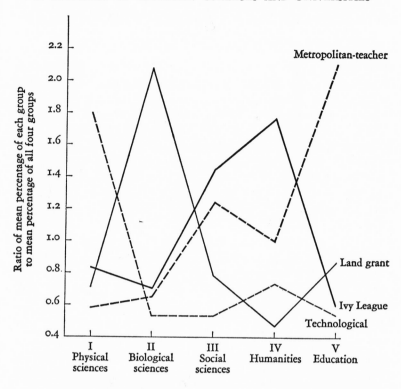

SOURCE: Robert H. Knapp and Linda A. Ehlinger, "Styles of Scholarly Production,"
Journal of Educational Research, LVI, 5 (1963), 249.

FIGURE I.

factor loadings in excess of +.85. Inspection of this listing will immediately reveal the heavy predominance of land grant institutions in the
Middle and Far West. It will also be noted that all are publicly supported, with the exception of Brigham Young and also Cornell, which,
being both publicly and privately sponsored, is a special case. Thus,
the second factor may be designated as a "land grant" factor.

The third factor is represented in Figure I by twelve institutions
with factor loadings in excess of +.75, as shown in Table 5. This
group of institutions is particularly weak in both physical and biological sciences and very strong in the field of education. Their contributions to the social sciences are clearly superior and their contributions

TABLE 3. Factor I—Ivy League
percentages in each of five areas.

Institution	I Physical Sciences	II Biological Sciences	III Social Sciences	IV Humanities	V Education
Chicago	34.6	16.2	29.3	11.7	8.2
Harvard	35.5	10.3	31.1	18.7	4.4
UCLA	30.3	15.2	32.4	9.0	13.1
Yale	37.6	8.6	29.2	19.5	5.1
State U. of Iowa	22.9	18.4	32.7	13.0	13.0
Dartmouth	29.1	14.4	29.1	18.8	8.6
North Carolina	29.4	13.5	27.3	20.2	9.6
Swarthmore	36.3	14.8	31.4	13.6	3.9
Virginia	36.4	11.0	26.8	21.0	4.8
Western Reserve	25.7	19.6	30.8	14.5	9.4
Amherst	27.1	7.8	33.7	24.0	7.4
Fordham	22.2	18.8	24.4	18.4	16.2
Duke	33.1	12.4	30.6	12.4	11.6
Wesleyan	29.1	12.6	27.4	22.6	8.3
St. Louis	28.3	10.8	31.4	20.6	9.0
MEAN	30.51	13.63	29.84	17.20	8.84

TABLE 4. Factor II—Land grant
percentages in each of five areas.

Institution	I Physical Sciences	II Biological Sciences	III Social Sciences	IV Humanities	V Education
Minnesota	29.4	28.3	21.3	7.5	13.3
Wisconsin	26.9	30.2	21.4	8.2	13.3
Cornell	34.7	35.3	16.5	6.3	7.2
Iowa U.	40.8	40.7	11.7	0.2	6.6
Nebraska	22.1	32.7	21.2	7.4	16.6
Missouri	22.7	27.3	20.4	9.2	20.4
Rutgers	29.7	39.3	12.5	5.2	13.3
Michigan State	21.6	52.6	13.9	2.9	9.0
Utah State	16.1	45.5	22.9	1.4	14.1
Brigham Young	18.2	38.1	16.4	7.7	19.6
Florida	29.8	28.2	20.5	5.3	16.2
Maryland	33.7	45.8	10.9	2.2	7.4
Kansas State	27.1	46.2	16.3	1.5	8.9
Massachusetts	17.6	64.6	9.4	4.1	4.4
LSU	30.6	31.6	16.8	7.1	13.8
Washington State	27.4	39.5	14.2	5.0	13.9
Oregon State	36.3	40.7	7.7	0.7	14.7

TABLE 4.

Institution	I Physical Sciences	II Biological Sciences	III Social Sciences	IV Humanities	V Education
Oklahoma State	15.6	49.4	13.0	3.3	18.6
Tennessee	27.9	30.7	17.7	5.6	18.1
Idaho	24.9	45.0	12.0	4.3	13.9
Texas A. & M.	39.4	42.3	11.3	0.0	7.0
Georgia	20.1	35.8	18.1	8.3	17.6
Connecticut	18.1	48.6	22.4	1.4	9.5
MEAN	26.55	39.93	16.02	4.56	12.93

TABLE 5. Factor III—Metropolitan-teacher percentages in each of five areas.

Institution	I Physical Sciences	II Biological Sciences	III Social Sciences	IV Humanities	V Education
NYU	25.5	12.6	23.0	10.4	28.5
Pittsburgh	26.5	17.1	25.8	8.4	22.2
Temple	29.2	12.9	25.8	7.4	24.6
Denver	17.7	14.6	29.2	9.7	28.8
Alabama	21.6	14.1	25.3	15.8	23.2
Ohio	29.3	14.9	26.0	4.2	25.6
Oregon	16.0	8.0	27.2	15.5	33.3
State C. of Iowa	9.6	8.6	23.4	4.6	53.8
Wayne State	29.2	12.8	24.9	12.3	20.8
Boston U.	10.7	8.4	28.5	17.6	34.8
USC	14.2	16.2	34.6	10.7	24.3
North Texas	21.2	12.9	14.7	6.0	45.2
MEAN	20.89	12.76	25.70	10.22	30.42

to the humanities substantial. There appear to be two types of institution included here, first, institutions located in metropolitan centers and subsequently sponsored by them, and second, teachers colleges or institutions that were formerly teachers colleges. It seems appropriate to describe this factor as "metropolitan-teacher."

The fourth factor is represented by nine institutions with factor loadings exceeding +.85, as shown in Table 6. The special attainments of this group are clearly in the physical sciences, though their contribution to the humanities appreciably exceeds that of the land grant institutions. In this group are a number of better-known engineering and scientific institutions such as Massachusetts Institute of Technology,

TABLE 6. Factor IV—Technological
percentages in each of five areas.

Institution	I Physical Sciences	II Biological Sciences	III Social Sciences	IV Humanities	V Education
MIT	89.7	6.4	2.8	0.2	0.9
Cal Tech	86.7	9.7	2.3	1.1	0.2
Johns Hopkins	55.1	13.9	14.7	8.7	7.6
Rochester	40.7	16.0	17.1	16.6	9.6
Carnegie Tech	85.5	1.4	2.6	3.1	7.4
Cincinnati	40.9	10.5	20.6	12.6	15.4
Notre Dame	54.3	9.3	15.8	13.4	7.3
Buffalo	41.9	14.5	19.0	7.3	17.3
RPI	91.3	5.4	0.8	0.0	2.5
MEAN	65.50	9.68	10.63	7.20	7.58

California Institute of Technology, Carnegie Institute of Technology, and Rensselaer Polytechnic Institute, as well as a number of institutions of strong technological leanings such as the University of Rochester, University of Buffalo, and Johns Hopkins University, among others. This factor may appropriately be called a "technological" factor.

We have then, in summary, identified four model styles of scholarly production among the ninety-five institutions most productive of graduates who have taken Ph.D.'s from 1936 to 1956. These are respectively an Ivy League, a land grant, a metropolitan-teacher, and a technological style. They differ radically in the pattern of their scholarly output and constitute, I believe, a valuable basis for evaluating the general character and intellectual climate of a particular institution. It may be profitable to examine one or two cases that are not included among those selected as most typical of our four factors. For example, the University of Pennsylvania, which is normally classified as an Ivy League institution, actually yields a higher loading on the technological factor than on the Ivy League factor because of its relatively high standing in the physical sciences. As such it constitutes a kind of hybrid. The same general pattern characterizes the University of Colorado, though it might commonly be assumed that these two institutions are profoundly different, as indeed they are in certain respects. Indiana University and the University of Washington are interesting because they have no distinguishing factor loadings, showing instead a moderate loading on all factors. They constitute a sort of "all-American" type of institution. Another institution of particular interest is

Catholic University, which yields a uniquely high negative loading on the land grant factor. This suggests that its pattern of scholarly attainments is antithetical to that of our land grant schools.

Thus, any of these ninety-five institutions may be evaluated with respect to our model styles of scholarly production. Fortunately we are not limited to the ninety-five most productive institutions. The report of the National Academy of Sciences gives the record for almost all other undergraduate institutions in the nation, and it is possible, by consulting these figures, to determine the degree to which any institution approximates each of these four styles or represents a hybrid of them.

It seems to me that this measure directly reflects the actual character of an institution, giving, for many purposes a more useful mode of classifying institutions than the more conventional categories mentioned earlier. Though the number of scholars produced by many institutions may be a small proportion of their total graduates, still the distribution of these scholars across the major fields of learning serves as a kind of pattern by which the intellectual climate of an institution may be discerned. Classification according to this typology, taken in conjunction with some measure of over-all productivity, that is, the ratio of scholars to graduates, offers, I believe, a very quick and meaningful picture of the institution as a whole.

This particular analysis was undertaken for a purpose more specific than simply devising a typology based upon scholarly output. I was concerned with identifying the type of institution in which the production of humanistic scholars constitutes a major area of achievement. The main result emerging from this chapter as it applies to my central purpose is the recognition that a fairly identifiable group of institutions, in which the private, wealthy eastern colleges predominate, seems to be a happy recruiting ground for the humanistic scholar. We shall find this conclusion persistently confirmed and shall later, in Chapters 9, 10, 11, 12, and 13, deal more extensively with the institutional factors that distinguish these institutions from the great state and land grant universities of the regions of the West—regions that, in most instances, have yet to attain distinction in the humanities comparable to their attainments in science, technology, and even the social sciences.

BACCALAUREATE ORIGINS

This chapter will examine the baccalaureate origins of the humanistic scholars listed in the roster of the National Academy of Sciences. It will be recalled that this roster includes all persons receiving doctorates from American universities in all fields from 1936 to 1959. The date of the bachelor's degree awarded these persons clearly extends considerably further back in time than 1936. In fact, some of those granted doctoral degrees in 1936 and afterward attained the baccalaureate degree during and even before World War I. Data have been obtained giving the baccalaureate years for all humanistic scholars on the roster of the National Academy of Sciences, and these have been assigned to four periods: Period I, extending to the baccalaureate class of 1925; Period II, including persons taking their baccalaureate from 1926 to 1935; Period III, from 1936 to 1945; and Period IV, from 1946 to 1959. Since my primary concern is with a contemporary evaluation of the origins of the American humanistic scholars, I shall disregard those persons receiving their B.A. before 1936, that is, Periods I and II. I have, on the other hand, considered Periods III and IV for examination here.

Initially, let us combine the five fields of humanistic scholarship in order to examine the number of institutions that contribute to the total number of humanistic scholars produced in the two periods. Male and female scholars will be separated, since the latter are comparatively few in number and will be dealt with as occasion requires. Table 7 shows the percentage of scholars produced in the humanities in Periods III and IV by increasingly larger portions of the total number of B.A.-granting institutions in the nation (which averaged about 1,200 in Period III and somewhat over 1,800 in Period IV). The striking aspect of Table 7 is the degree to which a comparatively small number of institutions in both periods produced the bulk of humanistic scholars from among their baccalaureates. Thus, ten institutions, and not necessarily the largest ones, account for the baccalaureate origins of between a quarter and a fifth of all humanistic scholars in both periods. There is strong reason to suppose, as we shall see, that the

TABLE 7. Production of male baccalaureates who
later received Ph.D.'s in humanities.

Period III

No. Institutions	No. Ph.D.'s	Per cent Ph.D.'s	Limit
top 10	1,035	22.4	66 or more
top 20	1,541	33.3	45 or more
top 30	1,890	40.9	30 or more
top 42	2,214	47.9	25 or more
top 59	2,590	56.0	19 or more
top 75	2,836	61.3	14 or more
top 102	3,144	68.0	10 or more
top 601	4,626	100.0	1 or more

Period IV

No. Institutions	No. Ph.D.'s	Per cent Ph.D.'s	Limit
top 10	929	24.1	59 or more
top 21	1,426	37.0	40 or more
top 30	1,694	44.0	28 or more
top 42	1,963	51.0	20 or more
top 61	2,286	59.4	16 or more
top 76	2,501	65.0	13 or more
top 102	2,768	71.9	9 or more
top 526	3,849	100.0	1 or more

quality of the scholars in this portion is higher than that in the remaining three-quarters. This table also shows that half of all humanistic scholars are produced by approximately forty-two institutions, or something less than 4 per cent of all institutions granting the baccalaureate degree. Earlier studies employing comparable data for the sciences (reported in *The Younger American Scholar*, 1953) show that the recruitment base is more diffuse and that the type of institution producing scientists tends to have a different character than that producing humanists.

The concentration of the baccalaureate origins of humanists seems, if anything, to be more marked in the more recent period (note "per cent Ph.D.'s" column). This may, however, be a statistical artifact, giving a deceivingly sharper concentration in the later period because in the larger and more productive universities the lapsed time between B.A. and Ph.D. is slightly less than in the more obscure institutions. On the other hand, there seems no suggestion that the baccalaureate origins of humanistic scholars have recently become more extended or diffuse. In fact, since the number of accredited undergraduate institutions has substantially increased from our third to our last period, the conclusion strongly suggested is that the humanists have not extended their recruitment base at the same rate that the American higher educational system has proliferated.

The concentration of origins for female scholars in the humanities is yet more extreme than that for males. Table 8 shows that the ten in-

TABLE 8. Production of female baccalaureates who
later received Ph.D.'s in humanities.

Period III

No. Institutions	No. Ph.D.'s	Per cent Ph.D.'s	Limit
top 10	212	22.5	14 or more
top 19	313	33.1	8 or more
top 34	410	43.5	6 or more
top 69	563	59.6	4 or more
top 326	943	100.0	1 or more

Period IV

No. Institutions	No. Ph.D.'s	Per cent Ph.D.'s	Limit
top 10	120	30.1	8 or more
top 23	184	46.2	4 or more
top 34	217	54.5	3 or more
top 67	283	71.0	2 or more
top 182	398	100.0	1 or more

stitutions most productive of female humanistic scholars in Period III account for almost one quarter of their number, while in Period IV the fraction is almost one third. Approximately seventy institutions in Period III account for 60 per cent of all female scholars, while a mere thirty-four institutions in our most recent period account for over fifty per cent. Thus the narrow recruitment base of female humanistic scholars is manifest here as in the case of the male scholars.

Table 9 lists institutions in the third period that, between 1936 and 1945, produced twenty or more male baccalaureates who later received a doctorate degree in the humanities. This list is of particular and immediate interest. It confirms the sharp recruitment concentration just discussed and further confirms the type of institution that breeds the humanistic scholar. Harvard, with 197 Ph.D.'s, heads the list; the University of Oklahoma, with 20 Ph.D.'s to its credit, concludes it. The latter number is equivalent to the modest yield of fewer

TABLE 9. Institutions producing 20 or more male
baccalaureates in Period III (1936-1945) who
later received Ph.D.'s in humanities.

Institution	No. Ph.D.'s	Institution	No. Ph.D.'s
Harvard	197	Missouri	30
California (Berkeley)	118	Williams	30
Yale	114	Cornell	29
CCNY	107	Virginia	29
Chicago	103	Haverford	28
Columbia	97	Boston U.	28
Princeton	93	Colorado	28
UCLA	71	Wesleyan	27
Illinois	69	Duke	27
Wisconsin	66	St. Louis	27
North Carolina	59	Brown	26
Catholic U.	57	Johns Hopkins	25
Michigan	56	Wayne State	25
Oberlin	54	Boston C.	25
Northwestern	51	Miami (Ohio)	24
NYU	47	Indiana	24
Brooklyn	46	Florida	24
Washington	46	Fordham	24
Texas	45	Utah	23
Amherst	45	Western Reserve	23
Dartmouth	43	Nebraska	23
Minnesota	42	Georgetown	23
Iowa U.	39	Kansas	22
Pennsylvania	35	Wooster	22
Stanford	34	DePauw	21
Rochester	33	Emory	21
Bowdoin	32	Oklahoma	20
Ohio State	31		

than two baccalaureates per year who continue to the doctorate in any
of our five humanistic fields.

This list, of course, was compiled without reference to institutional
size and the number of small, high-quality liberal arts colleges found
among this constricted list is notable. These include Oberlin in the
thirteenth position, and all of the so-called New England Pentagonal
colleges—Williams, Amherst, Wesleyan, Bowdoin, and Dartmouth—
despite the very small number of their graduates. But perhaps most
striking is the special eminence of the private universities such as Harvard, Yale, Princeton, Chicago, and Columbia, which are all found

among the first seven despite the comparatively small sizes of their baccalaureate classes.

This list includes a substantial number of the great state universities; the University of California, Berkeley, occupies the second position on the list, although its numerical record is substantially below that of Harvard. Of note also are such institutions as the University of California, Los Angeles, and the Universities of Illinois, Wisconsin, and North Carolina, all of which lie among the most productive dozen. It will be appreciated, however, that of the state universities standing fairly high on this list all have graduating classes many times the size of those of our larger, private universities. Moreover, the absolute number of scholars coming from these institutions, excepting Berkeley, is 40 per cent or less than those coming from Harvard in this period.

Among the remaining top-ranking institutions there are two rather special cases, one of which is the City College of New York, occupying fourth position and quite atypical among top-ranking institutions in terms of clientele and sponsorship. Nevertheless, CCNY's special excellence has emerged in other studies, and it is probably to be attributed to the peculiar and intense intellectual dedication of its student clientele. The second special case is Catholic University of America. In other studies, particularly those dealing with the origins of scientists, Roman Catholic institutions have appeared consistently unproductive. In the humanities, however, this foremost Catholic university is clearly of prominence. Chapter 9 will discuss this singular institution, and review more generally the position of the humanities in Catholic higher education.

The top-ranking institutions in the latest period, 1946-1959, are presented in Table 10. The first half-dozen schools, except for the University of California, Berkeley, are our principal private universities. Any displacements in rank position from the earlier period are probably without importance. The preponderance of eastern private, high-cost institutions is obvious, and there is no evidence that the recruitment base of humanities in this more recent period has been extended to a wider range or type of institutions, despite the postwar expansion of higher education. On balance, the two lists are remarkably similar.[1]

[1] I have established a lower limit of 20 for Period III and 16 for Period IV in order to obtain two lists of comparable length, Tables 9 and 10. It will be recalled that Period IV covers the baccalaureate years 1946-59, but since the median time for obtaining a doctorate in the humanities is approximately a decade, it is clear that many baccalaureates from these years have yet to attain the doctorate.

TABLE 10. Institutions producing 16 or more male
baccalaureates in Period IV (1946-1959) who
later received Ph.D.'s in humanities.

Institution	No. Ph.D.'s	Institution	No. Ph.D.'s
Harvard	181	Catholic U.	25
Yale	133	Boston U.	24
California (Berkeley)	106	USC	24
Chicago	106	Rutgers	22
Princeton	77	Washington U.	22
Columbia	73	Williams	22
NYU	67	Baylor	21
Wisconsin	67	Haverford	21
CCNY	60	Johns Hopkins	21
UCLA	59	Fordham	20
Michigan	57	Virginia	20
Brooklyn	52	Amherst	19
Washington	48	Denver	19
Pennsylvania	47	New Mexico	19
Texas	44	Colorado	18
Northwestern	43	Kansas	18
North Carolina	42	Michigan State	17
Stanford	41	Trinity	17
Illinois	41	Miami	17
Oberlin	40	Utah	17
Minnesota	40	Wesleyan	17
State U. of Iowa	35	Western Reserve	17
Indiana	31	Boston C.	16
Ohio State	30	Bowdoin	16
Queens	30	Emory	16
Dartmouth	29	George Washington	16
Wayne State	29	Alabama	16
Cornell	28	Missouri	16
Swarthmore	28	Nebraska	16
Syracuse	28	Vanderbilt	16
Rochester	27		

It may be interesting to examine in Table 11 a list showing the top-
ranking institutions for Periods III and IV, five or more of whose female baccalaureates have, as of 1959, attained the doctorate. This list,
like the others that precede it, makes no distinction with respect to the
size of the institution involved. The striking thing, of course, is the unusual prominence of small women's eastern colleges such as Bryn
Mawr, Vassar, Mount Holyoke, Smith, Radcliffe, and Wellesley. On
the other hand, the mass of state universities in the Mid-west and the

TABLE 11. Institutions producing 5 or more female
baccalaureates in Periods III and IV who later
received Ph.D.'s in humanities.

Period III

Institution	No. Ph.D.'s	Institution	No. Ph.D.'s
Bryn Mawr	32	Ohio State	7
Hunter	28	Wisconsin	7
Vassar	25	Agnes Scott	7
Columbia	20	Wilson	7
Mount Holyoke	20	Catholic U.	7
Smith	19	Fordham	6
Radcliffe	18	Duke	6
Chicago	18	Northwestern	6
Wellesley	17	New Rochelle	6
Minnesota	15	Wayne State	6
California (Berkeley)	14	St. Joseph's (Brooklyn)	6
UCLA	13	Marymount	5
NYU	12	Rockford	5
Manhattanville	12	Wooster	5
Brooklyn	12	Marquette	5
Swarthmore	11	Buffalo	5
Illinois	11	Pittsburgh	5
Texas	8	Washington	5
Stanford	8	Oklahoma	5
Boston U.	7	Goucher	5
Indiana	7	Western Reserve	5

Period IV

Institution	No. Ph.D.'s	Institution	No. Ph.D.'s
Hunter	22	Bryn Mawr	10
Wellesley	16	Radcliffe	8
Barnard	12	Brooklyn	7
Columbia	11	NYU	6
Smith	11	Oberlin	5
Swarthmore	10	Catholic U.	5
Vassar	10	Wisconsin	5
UCLA	10	Michigan	5

West make a very small contribution indeed, and the total number of
institutions yielding five or more in Period III is but forty-three, despite
the fact that all five of our fields of humanistic scholarship are included.
In Period IV, only sixteen institutions have produced five or more doctorates in the humanities, suggesting that a remarkably small number
of undergraduate institutions is responsible for female graduate stu-

dents in the humanities. The discrepancy between the number of institutions in the two lists perhaps results from the greater elapsed time between the B.A. and the Ph.D. degrees for female scholars. Evidence for this will be presented later.

It is now appropriate to examine the individual fields to determine whether any depart from the general trend already discussed. For the sake of simplicity, male and female scholars will be combined. Let us first consider foreign languages. Table 12 lists all institutions for Pe-

TABLE 12. Institutions producing 5 or more baccalaureates in Periods III and IV who later received Ph.D.'s in foreign languages and literature.

Period III

Institution	No. Ph.D.'s	Institution	No. Ph.D.'s
Harvard	47	Stanford	8
Columbia	31	Indiana	8
Yale	25	Ohio State	8
California (Berkeley)	25	Michigan	8
Chicago	23	Boston C.	8
CCNY	23	Brigham Young	7
Princeton	21	Reed	7
Illinois	20	Brown	7
UCLA	18	Pennsylvania	7
Hunter	14	Johns Hopkins	7
Washington	14	Colorado	7
Brooklyn	13	North Carolina	7
Texas	13	Iowa U.	7
Bowdoin	12	Washington U.	7
Catholic U.	12	Vassar	7
Bryn Mawr	12	Dartmouth	7
NYU	11	Davidson	6
Minnesota	11	DePauw	6
Virginia	10	Rutgers	6
Cornell	9	Missouri	6
Kansas	9	Wisconsin	6
Northwestern	9	Mount Holyoke	6
St. Louis	9	Radcliffe	6
Amherst	8	Wellesley	6
Haverford	8	Colgate	5
Oberlin	8	Wooster	5
Swarthmore	8	Lafayette	5
Fordham	8	Emory	5

TABLE 12.

Institution	No. Ph.D.'s	Institution	No. Ph.D.'s
Boston	5	Nebraska	5
Kentucky	5	Western Reserve	5
LSU	5	Miami (Ohio)	5
Duke	5	Wayne State	5
Cincinnati	5		

Period IV

Institution	No. Ph.D.'s	Institution	No. Ph.D.'s
Yale	34	State U. of Iowa	8
Harvard	30	Cornell	7
California (Berkeley)	30	Johns Hopkins	7
Chicago	23	Pittsburgh	7
Columbia	20	USC	7
Princeton	19	Haverford	7
Brooklyn	17	Oberlin	7
Hunter	17	Boston C.	6
CCNY	16	Boston U.	6
UCLA	15	Utah	6
Wisconsin	15	Indiana	6
NYU	14	Cincinnati	6
Ohio State	13	Trinity	6
Pennsylvania	12	Bryn Mawr	6
Michigan	11	Wayne State	6
Washington U.	11	Emory	5
Queens	10	New Mexico	5
North Carolina	10	Catholic U.	5
Texas	10	Minnesota	5
Bowdoin	8	Western Reserve	5

riods III and IV that have produced five or more baccalaureates continuing to the doctorate. Again, the eastern private universities are prominent among the high-ranking institutions. There is, indeed, a suggestion of greater concentration in Period IV than in Period III, but this may simply be a statistical artifact stemming from the different "lag times" for the graduates of different types of institutions. Surely there is no evidence that the field of significant contributors to this field of scholarship has increased in the postwar period.

Table 13 reveals the same facts in the field of history. The lists for Period III and Period IV show no particular variation from our composite lists save perhaps for the displacement of some of the smaller colleges, such as Amherst in Period IV, due perhaps to a more pro-

TABLE 13. Institutions producing 5 or more
baccalaureates in Periods III and IV who
later received Ph.D.'s in history.

Period III

Institution	No. Ph.D.'s	Institution	No. Ph.D.'s
Harvard	64	Nebraska	9
California (Berkeley)	64	Cornell	8
UCLA	44	Florida	8
CCNY	38	Washington and Lee	8
Yale	36	Oklahoma	8
Princeton	35	Rochester	8
Chicago	33	USC	8
Columbia	30	Smith	8
Wisconsin	28	Maine	8
Illinois	24	Vassar	8
Stanford	21	Wayne State	8
Texas	21	Boston C.	8
Amherst	20	Bowdoin	7
Minnesota	20	Occidental	7
North Carolina	19	Swarthmore	7
Dartmouth	17	St. John's U.	7
Brooklyn	15	Emory	7
Michigan	15	Wheaton	7
Oberlin	14	Brown	7
Colorado U.	14	Miami (Ohio)	7
Indiana	14	Southwest Missouri	7
Iowa U.	13	Baylor	7
Virginia	13	Gonzaga	6
Duke	13	Hampden-Sydney	6
Ohio State	13	Knox	6
Catholic U.	12	Reed	6
St. Louis	12	Richmond	6
NYU	11	Utah	6
Johns Hopkins	11	LSU	6
Washington U.	11	Bryn Mawr	6
Missouri	11	Vermont	6
Northwestern	11	Augustana (Ill.)	5
Williams	10	Bates	5
Western Reserve	10	DePauw	5
Southern Illinois	10	Gettysburg	5
Wooster	9	Grinnell	5
Boston U.	9	Haverford	5
Wesleyan	9	Loyola	5
George Washington	9	Muhlenberg	5
Pittsburgh	9	Wake Forest	5
Georgetown	9	Rutgers	5

27

BACCALAUREATE ORIGINS

TABLE 13.

Institution	No. Ph.D.'s	Institution	No. Ph.D.'s
Cincinnati	5	Central Missouri	5
Washington U.	5	Nebraska State	5
Mount Holyoke	5	Southeast Missouri	5

Period IV

Institution	No. Ph.D.'s	Institution	No. Ph.D.'s
Harvard	61	State U. of Iowa	7
Yale	43	Nebraska	7
California (Berkeley)	38	St. Louis	7
CCNY	25	Trinity	7
Columbia	25	Arkansas	7
Princeton	25	Alabama	7
Wisconsin	25	Oregon	7
Chicago	23	Wellesley	7
UCLA	23	Miami (Ohio)	7
Stanford	22	Albany	6
NYU	19	State C. of Iowa	6
Illinois	19	Wesleyan	6
Washington	18	Williams	6
Brooklyn	17	Smith	6
Swarthmore	17	Roosevelt	6
Michigan	17	Brown	6
Rutgers	13	Tulane	6
Pennsylvania	13	Johns Hopkins	6
Syracuse	12	Fordham	6
Texas	12	Colorado U.	6
Minnesota	12	Vanderbilt	6
Oberlin	12	Kansas	6
Dartmouth	12	DePauw	6
Baylor	12	Emory	5
Indiana	11	Temple	5
Ohio State	11	Duke	5
Wayne State	11	Western Reserve	5
North Carolina	10	Amherst	5
Cornell	8	Wooster	5
Michigan State	8	Gonzaga	5
Rochester	8	Haverford	5
Georgetown	8	Pomona	5
Washington U.	8	SMU	5
Northwestern	8	Wheaton	5
Carleton	8	California (Santa Barbara)	5
Boston U.	7	William and Mary	5
George Washington	7	Queens	5
New Mexico	7	Auburn	5
USC	7		

28

tracted "lag period" between the baccalaureate and the doctoral degrees for graduates of smaller institutions.

For the field of English, Table 14 presents the top institutions for Periods III and IV. With monotonous regularity Harvard and other Ivy League institutions head the list. In both periods the University of Chicago attains unusual prominence; in Period III the University of North Carolina is notable in its fourth position. But the general character of the list and the ordering of the institutions are remarkably similar to those observed for the fields of history and foreign languages.

TABLE 14. Institutions producing 5 or more
baccalaureates in Periods III and IV who
later received Ph.D.'s in English.

Period III

Institution	No. Ph.D.'s	Institution	No. Ph.D.'s
Harvard	51	Miami (Ohio)	11
Chicago	40	Kansas	11
Yale	39	Wayne State	11
North Carolina	32	Bowdoin	10
CCNY	30	Brigham Young	10
Columbia	27	Wooster	10
Princeton	27	Haverford	10
California (Berkeley)	26	Wesleyan	10
Illinois	23	Williams	10
Brooklyn	22	Fordham	9
Washington U.	21	Stanford	9
NYU	20	Ohio State	9
Pennsylvania	20	Pittsburgh	9
Wisconsin	20	Mount Holyoke	9
Michigan	18	Western Reserve	9
State U. of Iowa	17	Swarthmore	8
Minnesota	16	Massachusetts	8
Texas	16	Duke	8
Amherst	15	Indiana	8
Cornell	14	Loyola	8
Northwestern	14	Oklahoma	8
Vanderbilt	14	Notre Dame	8
Dartmouth	14	Furman	7
Missouri	14	St. John's U.	7
UCLA	13	Hamilton	7
Florida	13	Middlebury	7
Boston U.	12	Penn State	7
Oberlin	12	Louisville	7
Brown	11	Utah	7

TABLE 14.

Institution	No. Ph.D.'s	Institution	No. Ph.D.'s
Catholic U.	7	Franklin and Marshall	5
Johns Hopkins	7	Lafayette	5
Temple	7	Maryville	5
Hunter	7	Reed	5
Cornell	6	Kansas City	5
Emory	6	Buffalo	5
Wabash	6	South Carolina	5
George Washington	6	Georgetown	5
Kentucky	6	Syracuse	5
Rochester	6	Colorado U.	5
Virginia	6	Smith	5
St. Louis	6	Vassar	5
Bates	5	Baylor	5
Holy Cross	5	Texas Tech	5

Period IV

Institution	No. Ph.D.'s	Institution	No. Ph.D.'s
Harvard	58	Williams	10
Chicago	38	Queens	10
Yale	31	Syracuse	9
California (Berkeley)	30	Vanderbilt	9
NYU	29	Indiana	9
Columbia	24	Kansas	9
Princeton	23	Miami	9
Brooklyn	22	Dartmouth	8
Michigan	22	New Mexico	8
Wisconsin	20	Boston U.	8
Northwestern	18	Colorado U.	8
North Carolina	18	Oregon	8
Texas	18	Notre Dame	8
UCLA	16	Loyola	8
Illinois	15	Washington U.	8
Minnesota	14	Wayne State	7
Washington	14	Florida	7
Pennsylvania	13	Tennessee	7
Cornell	12	Brown	7
Oberlin	12	Stanford	7
Swarthmore	12	Kenyon	7
CCNY	12	Baylor	6
Missouri	11	Wesleyan	6
Oklahoma	11	Wofford	6
Amherst	10	Alabama	6
Holy Cross	10	Tulsa	6
State U. of Iowa	10	Union	6

TABLE 14.

Institution	No. Ph.D.'s	Institution	No. Ph.D.'s
TCU	6	Penn State	5
Emory	6	Rutgers	5
Johns Hopkins	6	Tulane	5
Michigan State	6	Maryland	5
Utah	6	Pittsburgh	5
Duke	6	Rochester	5
LSU	6	Virginia	5
Ohio State	6	Nebraska	5
Western Reserve	6	Catholic U.	5
DePauw	6	Temple	5
Haverford	6	St. John's U.	5

Significant contributors to the field of philosophy, as shown in Table 15, are fewer in number than those to history, English, or foreign languages in both Periods III and IV. This fact probably reflects in part the comparatively small numbers in this field. Still, only twenty institutions yielded five or more baccalaureates continuing to the doctorate in Period IV, while twenty-four institutions yielded a similar number in Period III. Of all the humanistic disciplines, excepting the fine arts, it appears that philosophy has the most constricted recruitment base. Philosophy seems to be more than usually dependent upon private, high-cost universities and Roman Catholic institutions for the recruitment of its membership.

There remains to be discussed only the field of fine arts and music. Table 16 shows the singular position of Oberlin in Period III, reflecting the special development of its music conservatory. Beyond this, the list contains few surprises, save perhaps for the unique position of the State University of Iowa in Period IV. We shall have occasion elsewhere in this book to look more closely at this institution, which departs in a number of basic aspects from public and other land grant universities in its support of the arts and literature. There is a significant tendency in Period IV for the number of productive institutions to be sharply reduced. Thus, nineteen institutions produced five or more baccalaureates (one every two years) who have subsequently earned the doctorate in Period III. For Period IV the number of institutions stands at only twelve. Allowing for statistical artifact, it is still plain that the recruitment base for doctorates in these fields is surely not broadening, and may, indeed, be more constricted in the most recent

TABLE 15. Institutions producing 5 or more
baccalaureates in Periods III and IV who
later received Ph.D.'s in philosophy.

Period III

Institution	No. Ph.D.'s	Institution	No. Ph.D.'s
Catholic U.	33	Brooklyn	6
Columbia	19	Princeton	6
Chicago	17	Yale	6
Harvard	16	Georgetown	5
California (Berkeley)	13	Haverford	5
CCNY	11	Marquette	5
Fordham	9	Boston U.	5
Michigan	8	Wesleyan	5
Bryn Mawr	7	Duke	5
Loyola	7	UCLA	5
NYU	7	Boston C.	5
Minnesota	7	Northwestern	5

Period IV

Institution	No. Ph.D.'s	Institution	No. Ph.D.'s
Chicago	22	Princeton	8
Harvard	17	Stanford	7
Catholic U.	16	UCLA	7
Columbia	12	Minnesota	7
Yale	11	Pennsylvania	7
Oberlin	10	NYU	6
Wisconsin	10	California (Berkeley)	6
Virginia	9	Michigan	6
Fordham	8	Northwestern	5
CCNY	8	Swarthmore	5

period. As in the field of philosophy, scholars in the arts are recruited
from a very small number of institutions.

Apart from intrinsic interest of the above lists, one or two further
observations should be made. Clearly the number of institutions producing baccalaureates who continue on to the doctorate is remarkably
small. *The Younger American Scholar* (1953) by Knapp and Greenbaum, concluded that the recruitment base for the humanities was pe-
culiarly narrow as compared to that of the sciences. There is nothing in
the present data that qualifies or attenuates that earlier verdict. Of the
several disciplines, it appears that history and English, which claim a
numerically greater number of students have a relatively wide base of
recruitment. The disciplines with the most tenuous hold upon the in-

TABLE 16. Institutions producing 5 or more
baccalaureates in Periods III and IV who
later received Ph.D.'s in fine arts
and music.

Period III

Institution	No. Ph.D.'s	Institution	No. Ph.D.'s
Oberlin	21	Chicago	8
Harvard	19	Ohio State	7
Northwestern	18	Nebraska	6
Rochester	17	Carnegie Tech	5
Wisconsin	16	CCNY	5
Columbia	10	Wellesley	5
NYU	10	Princeton	5
Illinois	10	State U. of Iowa	5
Michigan	9	Utah	5
Yale	9		

Period IV

Institution	No. Ph.D.'s	Institution	No. Ph.D.'s
Harvard	15	USC	8
Yale	14	Indiana	6
State U. of Iowa	11	Michigan	6
Rochester	11	NYU	5
Northwestern	10	Queens	5
UCLA	8	California (Berkeley)	5

tellectual imagination of the American college population are philosophy and the fine arts. The latter is a newly developed field, in which doctorates have only recently been granted. Also, the relative unpopularity of philosophy may possibly be explained by the fact that contemporary logical and analytic philosophy seems to be formidable and esoteric, whereas the history of philosophy is subsumed in such fields as history, theology, literature, and others. But there is no question about philosophy's very ancient and honorable ancestry as a scholarly discipline. The narrowness of its recruitment base constitutes a severe indictment of our system of higher education.

At this juncture it would be illuminating to report the results of an analysis quite relevant to our subject. The ratio of the number of baccalaureates taking doctorates in the sciences to the number taking doctorates in the humanities from 1936 to 1956 (National Academy of Sciences, 1958) indicates in a very important manner the direction of the intellectual thrust of different institutions. Accordingly, Table 17

TABLE 17. Institutions most productive of
baccalaureates who received Ph.D.'s in Period IV.

Institution	Scientist-Humanist Ratio	Ph.D.'s in Humanities	Institution	Scientist-Humanist Ratio	Ph.D.'s in Humanities
1. Catholic U.	.4	136	42. Brown	3.3	63
2. Boston U.	.8	73	43. George Washington	3.3	49
3. Amherst	.9	104	44. North Texas	3.5	21
4. Oregon	1.0	51	45. Oklahoma	3.6	45
5. St. Louis	1.2	74	46. Reed	3.6	36
6. Princeton	1.2	225	47. Colorado	3.9	36
7. Hunter	1.2	77	48. Missouri	3.9	73
8. Wesleyan	1.3	75	49. Temple	3.9	35
9. Alabama	1.4	62	50. Washington	3.9	119
10. North Carolina	1.5	113	51. Notre Dame	3.9	40
11. Yale	1.5	274	52. Kansas	4.0	66
12. Dartmouth	1.5	114	53. Michigan	4.1	184
13. Columbia	1.6	309	54. CCNY	4.3	232
14. Harvard	1.6	440	55. Georgia	4.6	25
15. State C. of Iowa	1.7	21	56. Wisconsin	4.6	200
16. Virginia	1.7	80	57. California		
17. Oberlin	1.8	158	(Berkeley)	4.6	303
18. Fordham	1.8	59	58. Brooklyn	4.8	93
19. Wooster	1.9	57	59. Johns Hopkins	4.9	60
20. USC	2.0	47	60. Nebraska	5.0	65
21. Emory	2.1	59	61. Syracuse	5.3	44
22. Duke	2.2	50	62. Minnesota	5.4	157
23. Northwestern	2.2	129	63. Buffalo	5.8	24
24. Western Reserve	2.3	55	64. Arkansas	5.9	20
25. Stanford	2.3	139	65. Kentucky	5.9	33
26. State U. of Iowa	2.3	108	66. LSU	6.2	30
27. Wayne State	2.4	60	67. Utah	6.2	48
28. Swarthmore	2.4	70	68. Ohio State	6.2	100
29. Pennsylvania	2.4	141	69. Brigham Young	6.3	30
30. Denver	2.4	30	70. Ohio	6.3	15
31. Rochester	2.5	81	71. Florida	7.0	31
32. Texas	2.6	150	72. Illinois	7.2	160
33. UCLA	2.8	157	73. Tennessee	7.4	17
34. Cincinnati	2.9	50	74. Cornell	8.4	94
35. Miami (Ohio)	3.0	54	75. Rutgers	8.9	42
36. Chicago	3.1	279	76. West Virginia	9.4	19
37. DePauw	3.2	57	77. Washington State	11.1	17
38. Indiana	3.2	76	78. Idaho	12.2	12
39. Pittsburgh	3.2	75	79. Penn State	13.7	41
40. Washington U.	3.2	55	80. New Hampshire	14.5	11
41. NYU	3.2	146	81. Oklahoma State	15.9	11

TABLE 17.

Institution	Scientist-Humanist Ratio	Ph.D.'s in Humanities	Institution	Scientist-Humanist Ratio	Ph.D.'s in Humanities
82. Michigan State	16.0	22	89. Purdue	"	7
83. Massachusetts	16.4	16	90. Texas A & M	"	2
84. Maryland	19.1	13	91. Cal Tech	"	5
85. Connecticut	Exceeds 20.0	6	92. Iowa U.	"	5
86. Utah State	"	9	93. Oregon State	"	2
87. Carnegie Tech	"	11	94. MIT	"	2
88. Kansas State	"	8	95. RPI	"	0

lists the ninety-five institutions whose baccalaureates received the greatest number of doctorates between 1936 and 1956. The ratio of scientists to humanists has been calculated. The figures for the humanities are taken, of course, from our five fields; those for the sciences are taken from combined figures for the biological and physical sciences, including mathematics but excluding the so-called social sciences. The first column shows the ratio described; the second lists the total number of baccalaureates who have taken the doctorate in the humanities during this span.

Perhaps the first observation to be made is that low ratios tend, with some outstanding exceptions, to be characteristic of the private, eastern colleges and universities, and that our major eastern Ivy League universities are all found among the first fourteen institutions. Also included here are such eastern high-cost liberal arts colleges as Amherst, Wesleyan, and Dartmouth. Moving down the list, private eastern institutions become relatively scarce, and the incidence of state and land grant colleges steadily increases. The list ends with a group of institutions devoted primarily to science and technology. We shall have occasion later on to consider this ratio, particularly in comparison to Ivy League with state universities. It should be clear, even at this juncture, however, that with a few exceptions the larger state universities yield many more scientists than humanists. City colleges, eastern Ivy League universities, high-quality liberal arts colleges, and Catholic institutions show only a slight preponderance of scientists over humanists, on the average.

⋖§ 4 ξ⋗

A SAMPLE OF LIBERAL ARTS COLLEGES

In this chapter and the next, institutions shall be evaluated not in terms of the absolute number of baccalaureates who continue to the doctoral degree in humanities, but rather in terms of a rate of doctorates per thousand baccalaureates. Exceptional merit may thus be recognized in certain smaller institutions. Such procedure, although perhaps open to criticism, is a valuable supplement to the preceding chapter, which in dealing with absolute numbers obscures the fact that some of our more productive institutions harbor vast student bodies, while others have very constricted numbers.

We are dealing here with the output of male humanistic scholars only, since the number of females in the humanities is usually small, as we have observed; also, computation of any index, or rate per thousand graduates, among coeducational institutions would be complicated and involved if females were included. For our Period III (the years 1939 through 1945), precise male baccalaureate figures for two years, 1939 and 1943, were obtained; this two-year sum was multiplied by 5 for a reasonable estimate of the total number of male graduates over a decade span.

The estimate of the total number of graduates for Period IV (the years 1946 through 1959) involved some more subtle calculations. Since the average time between the baccalaureate and the doctoral degree in the humanities is approximately a decade, it would be patently in error to estimate the total number of male graduates from 1946 through 1959 as a basis for the computation of the humanities index, since it is evident that the closer the baccalaureate date approaches our terminal year of 1959, the more unlikely it becomes that a graduate of the institution may have earned his doctorate. Instead of accounting for this by giving older classes more weight in the final totals, it was simpler and equally valid to find empirically what fraction of the total for the fourteen-year period was "effective," by excluding people who could not fairly be included. After examination of representative institutions, it was found that 5/14 of the total number of male graduates between 1946 and 1959 could be validly included. This fraction was

36

obtained by multiplying a representative annual male class by 5 (since each year represents about 1/14). In the end this was done indirectly, by summing up the number of male baccalaureates for each institution in the class of 1949 and the class of 1953, and multiplying the sum of these two classes by 2.5, to secure an estimate of the "effective" male graduates for Period IV.

Accordingly, for every institution, a humanistic index was computed, expressing the rate per "effective" thousand at which the male baccalaureate population had obtained the doctorate in humanities. Beyond this, partial indices giving the rate per thousand for our five areas of the humanities were computed. One further observation should be made. There is no indication in this data of the quality of the humanistic scholar produced by each institution. We are necessarily confined to the number of doctorates received in the humanities by their graduates. Elsewhere, especially in viewing recruitment of major graduate schools, there will be evidence that the more prestigious universities draw their graduate students from undergraduate institutions of comparable prestige and type. I shall also show that those awarded fellowships from the American Council of Learned Societies, presumably an elite group among humanistic scholars, tend to have their baccalaureate origins heavily concentrated in a small number of famous private universities. Thus, it seems improbable that there are not important differences in the quality of humanistic students from different undergraduate institutions.

First, let us examine a list of institutions whose production of humanistic scholars per thousand male graduate students exceeds a rate of 10.0. These may be described as having a very high yield of humanistic scholars in proportion to the number of their graduates. Table 18

TABLE 18. High male indices of production (number of humanist scholars per thousand baccalaureates) in Periods III and IV.

Period III

Haverford	43.4	Chicago	24.0
Oberlin	36.1	Harvard	23.8
Catholic U.	34.4	Wesleyan	22.1
Bowdoin	28.6	Williams	20.2
Wooster	26.5	Princeton	19.4
Swarthmore	26.2	Rochester	17.6
Amherst	25.7	Middlebury	17.6

37

TABLE 18.

Wabash	16.1	Virginia	11.9
Hamilton	15.1	Dickinson	11.8
Occidental	14.6	Murray State	11.8
St. Louis	14.4	Colby	11.5
Hampden-Sydney	13.7	Gonzaga	11.5
UCLA	13.4	St. Olaf	11.2
DePauw	13.3	Yale	10.6
Gettysburg	12.7	Furman	10.6
Wheaton	12.6	Wofford	10.5
North Carolina	12.6	Johns Hopkins	10.5
Bates	12.4	Davidson	10.4
Columbia	12.4	Illinois Wesleyan	10.2
Southwest Missouri	12.4	Brown	10.1
Grinnell	12.1		

Period IV

Swarthmore	49.7	Trinity	15.8
Chicago	44.0	Amherst	15.7
Haverford	39.6	Williams	15.4
Oberlin	37.6	DePauw	15.3
Grinnell	31.4	Hiram	15.2
Kenyon	30.0	Randolph-Macon	15.2
Carleton	28.6	Yeshiva	14.0
Queens	28.2	Johns Hopkins	13.9
Harvard	27.8	Rockhurst	13.8
Albany	27.2	Bowdoin	13.7
Calvin	24.3	Clark	13.4
Princeton	21.5	Augustana (S.D.)	13.4
Catholic U.	21.5	Wofford	13.2
Birmingham-Southern	20.7	Wabash	12.7
Wesleyan	19.9	Brooklyn	12.4
Pomona	19.3	Augustana (Ill.)	12.4
Hamilton	19.1	Antioch	11.5
Wooster	18.6	New Mexico	11.3
Yale	18.3	Mount Union	10.9
Peabody	17.3	Vanderbilt	10.8
Rochester	16.9	John Carroll	10.3
Sewanee	16.7	Stanford	10.2
Rollins	16.4	Wheaton (Ill.)	10.2
Colorado	16.4		

presents this list for Periods III and IV for all institutions having an estimated total number of male graduates of six hundred or more during the span of years under consideration. Some institutions are not reported here because of the great statistical unreliability of their index.

It will be seen that nearly all high-ranking institutions are privately controlled and that there is here a heavy weighting of Ivy League universities and eastern liberal arts colleges. But included also are several city colleges such as Brooklyn and Queens, and one state university, the University of New Mexico. One should observe that the rate falls off very rapidly as one proceeds down the list of these most productive institutions. This points up the fact that regardless of whether absolute numbers or our humanistic indices are considered, the concentration of institutions contributing to the ranks of the humanistic fraternity rests upon a particularly narrow base. Also, the list for the fourth period is only slightly longer than for the third despite the great burgeoning of American higher education in the past two decades. Thus it appears that there is no marked tendency for the humanistic fraternity to greatly expand its recruitment base.

Further consideration of this humanistic index, particularly as it relates to such variables as type, cost, and location of institution, can probably not be carried out effectively without the selection of particular samples of institutions. For this reason, the rest of this chapter will report on the performance of two samples of liberal arts colleges. The first sample, covering Period III, consists of those private, liberal arts institutions annually graduating more than sixty males but fewer than two hundred, on the average, between 1936 and 1945. The second sample, covering Period IV, to a very large extent replicates the first sample and comprises those liberal arts institutions that had similar numbers of male graduates for the immediate postwar period. Although most schools in the first sample are also in the second, the number of smaller institutions that expanded after the war makes the second sample larger.

Tables 19 through 22 consider the ninety liberal arts colleges in Period III with respect to several variables. The first variable against which we compare these indices is that of geographic location. The average partial indices are given in Table 19, showing what part of a geographical region's total Ph.D. production each humanistic field is responsible for. Several kinds of comparisons may be made from this table.

TABLE 19. Average male index (college)
in Period III, by field and region.

	9^a New England	24 Mid-Atlantic	19 South	31 Midwest	7 West
Foreign languages and literature	3.1^b	1.6	1.1	1.0	1.2
History	5.0	1.7	2.6	2.3	3.1
English	5.2	2.1	2.4	2.2	2.1
Fine arts and music	0.4	0.03	0.3	1.5	0.4
Philosophy	1.5	0.7	0.3	0.7	0.9
TOTAL	15.1	6.2	6.7	7.7	7.8

[a] Number of institutions.
[b] Rate of Ph.D.'s per thousand baccalaureates.

A remarkable concentration of high effectiveness exists among the nine New England liberal arts institutions. The New England average is more than twice that of any other region, except the West, and only slightly less than twice the average indices of the West itself. Beyond this, we see that in general this pattern applies to all fields of humanistic scholarship except fine arts and music, in which field the partial indices are excessively small, although a comparatively high productivity in the Midwest is suggested. Western institutions turn in a creditable performance in history, especially when compared with the Middle Atlantic institutions, whereas the opposite pattern obtains with respect to foreign languages and literature. The study of foreign language and literature along the North Atlantic seaboard may be partly facilitated by the relatively high density of recent European bilingual immigrants, and distinguished library facilities not available elsewhere. In the main, however, New England's sharp ascendance over other geographic regions seems quite consistently established, whereas the Midwest, which my other studies previously cited have demonstrated to be so productive of scientists, shows a very indifferent yield of humanists.

The next variable examined was the cost of attendance. The figure used here was obtained from *American Universities and Colleges*[1] for

[1] A. J. Brumbaugh, ed., *American Universities and Colleges* (American Council on Education, 1940).

the years 1936 and 1940, and included costs of tuition, room, and board. Based on the average for these two years, the institutions were divided as nearly as possible into five ascending cost groups. For each of these cost groups the average partial index (as in Table 19) and average total humanistic index (as in Table 18) were computed, to yield the results presented in Table 20. Again, a fairly consistent picture emerges: a tendency for the average index of production to remain stable throughout our first four cost brackets, and then to rise sharply in the top cost bracket. Clearly, this is the general picture for foreign languages and literature, fine arts and music, and philosophy. History, on the other hand, shows a more even spread across the five categories, and English paradoxically shows an elevation in the lowest cost category, causing it to stand second only to the uppermost. The significance of these departures from the general trend and their reliability is not entirely clear.

TABLE 20. Average male index (college) in Period III, by field and cost of attendance.

	18[a] $0-425	19 $426-524	18 $525-600	18 $601-725	17 $726-1,000
Foreign languages and literature	0.9[b]	1.2	1.4	1.0	2.5
History	2.4	2.1	2.4	2.4	3.3
English	3.0	1.7	1.9	2.5	3.5
Fine arts and music	0.6	0.6	0.3	0.3	1.1
Philosophy	0.3	0.5	0.9	0.6	1.2
TOTAL	7.3	6.1	7.7	6.7	10.9

[a] Number of institutions.
[b] Rate of Ph.D.'s per thousand baccalaureates.

The main trend, showing the high productivity of our most costly liberal arts institutions, is quite inconsistent with the results obtained for the origins of scientists in my studies made with H. B. Goodrich (1952) and with Joseph J. Greenbaum (1953). The top cost bracket is not notably productive of the origins of scientists, and in the years prior to World War II it was clearly less productive than the moderate cost brackets.

The next variable examined was the type of administrative control. Using *American Universities and Colleges* (1940) again as a reference source, I divided the entire sample into three groups, those of

Catholic, Protestant, and nondenominational control. The separation between Protestant and nondenominational institutions is of course, somewhat arbitrary; many so-called Protestant institutions have such tenuous affiliation with the sponsoring church that they are, in effect, nondenominational. Still, I have preserved here the classification assigned to them in the source cited—one to which they, themselves, subscribed. Table 21 sets forth the results of this analysis.

TABLE 21. Average male index (college) in Period III, by field and type of administrative control.

	23[a] Catholic	42 Protestant	25 Nondenominational
Foreign languages and literature	0.5[b]	1.5	2.3
History	1.0	2.8	3.5
English	1.1	2.7	3.5
Fine arts and music	0.1	0.7	0.9
Philosophy	0.8	0.6	0.8
TOTAL	3.5	8.4	11.2

a Number of institutions.
b Rate of Ph.D.'s per thousand baccalaureates.

Immediately one sees that Catholic institutions are on an average, least productive, while the nondenominational institutions are most productive in every category. How much importance should be attached to the singularly low standing of Catholic institutions in fine arts and music, in contrast to their relatively high standing in philosophy? Philosophy in Catholic education has retained a degree of centrality in the curriculum, a fact well illustrated in Chapter 10's discussion of Catholic University of America. The almost total absence of a contribution to fine arts and music poses an interesting question that shall not be pursued further at this time. However, this quality of Catholic higher education is also manifest in more recent times, and suggests an almost calculated neglect of these scholarly areas. Any distinction between the performance of Protestant and nondenominational liberal arts institutions deserves no particular comment. In the main, the rates of production for each of the five humanistic fields are approximately the same.

I might add, in conclusion, that the type of administrative control is by no means independent of geographic location or cost of attendance.

Of the highly productive eastern liberal arts colleges, few have any present religious affiliation, although virtually all were founded by a religious body. Institutions of Protestant religious affiliation tend to be located in the Midwest and the South, to be of more modest cost, and to be less exclusive in their selection of students, serving, as they do, as educational organs for their constituency. This is also true of Catholic institutions which rarely maintain high standards of admission or high cost of attendance. Catholic colleges, however, tend to be concentrated in centers of population.

We are dealing here only with male humanistic scholars as a proportion of the male graduates of these colleges. But the majority of these institutions are coeducational, and, thirty-eight of them are exclusively for men. It is interesting, therefore, to note the average index of Ph.D. production for men's liberal arts colleges stands at 8.9, while that for coeducational institutions is 7.1. On the surface this difference is small, and suggests the relative unimportance of coeducation as a correlate of the output of humanists. Closer inspection, however, shows that if our institutions are divided into Catholic and non-Catholic, while preserving the categories of "male" and "coeducational," we obtain the results shown in Table 22.

TABLE 22. Average male index (college) in Period III, by male and coeducational as well as Catholic and non-Catholic types.

Male vs. Coed Total		Male vs. Coed Total by Affiliation			
		Male Total		Coed Total	
38[a]	52	18	20	5	47
Male	Coed	Cath.	Non-Cath.	Cath.	Non-Cath.
8.9[b]	7.1	4.4	12.1	1.7	8.3

[a] Number of institutions.
[b] Rate of Ph.D.'s per thousand baccalaureates.

The most productive group is conspicuously the non-Catholic men's institutions; least productive are the Catholic coeducational institutions. Again, non-Catholic coeducational schools exceed by almost 50 per cent the average productivity of men's Catholic institutions. This table clearly illustrates how the humanistic index may be correlated for two different factors simultaneously. It is clear that in Ph.D. productivity the non-Catholic institution is rated over the Catholic institution; but in addition, there is good evidence that men's insitutions

43

are more productive than coeducational institutions. Thus, the apparently equal averages of men's and coeducational colleges are misleading and must be examined in this light.

The next group of tables, 23 through 26, concerns a liberal arts sample for the fourth period. As noted earlier, the number of institutions qualifying for admission to our liberal arts sample has increased by a margin of approximately 50 per cent in the postwar era, due to the expansion of the smaller and previously obscure colleges into the size bracket meeting our criterion. Whereas Period III was based on a sample of 90 colleges, Period IV is based on a sample of 154. The sample for Period IV, since it is both more recent and more complete, therefore presents a statistically more accurate analysis of the manner in which Ph.D. production in the humanities is related to various independent factors. We shall begin, as before, with a consideration of the geographic location, using the same categories as those previously described. Table 23 shows the average partial index for the five fields un-

TABLE 23. Average male index (college)
in Period IV, by field and region.

	10[a] New England	35 Mid- Atlantic	32 South	60 Midwest	17 West
Foreign languages and literature	2.2[b]	1.1	0.9	1.1	0.4
History	3.5	1.8	1.7	3.0	2.7
English	4.8	2.0	2.3	2.2	1.4
Fine arts and music	0.8	0.1	0.3	0.6	0.8
Philosophy	1.0	0.7	0.7	1.2	0.7
TOTAL	12.2	5.7	5.9	8.0	6.1

[a] Number of institutions.
[b] Rate of Ph.D.'s per thousand baccalaureates.

der consideration, as well as the average total index for each of the five regions. Once again, the sharp superiority of New England over other geographic regions is established; this region is again almost twice as productive as any of the remaining four in its average total index. This pattern is generally and quite clearly sustained in the fields of English, foreign languages and literature, and history, although with some unevenness in the last of these. Fine arts and music, which represents a very small area, yields an inherently unstable partial index and offers no occasion for interpretation. The gradient

44

for philosophy does not correspond to the general humanistic gradient, but here, again, the field is small and the indices essentially unstable. There is a suggestion that the Midwest is improving its relative position in this most recent period, especially in the fields of history and philosophy. In the next chapter's consideration of universities, where the numbers involved are substantially greater, we shall explore this suggested trend further.

Let us now consider the cost categories. Once again the sample is divided into five approximately equal groups, dependent upon their annual cost of attendance as set forth for two years (1948 and 1952) in *American Colleges and Universities*. The general and partial indices for the five cost groups are set forth in Table 24. It should come as no surprise that the limits of each cost category have moved upward in the postwar era. The most costly fifth, however, is more than twice as productive, on the average, as each of the remaining four-fifths. In fact, the lowest four-fifths are remarkably uniform, with a rate of slightly over 5 per 1,000, while the top fifth falls just short of 12 per 1,000. In comparison with the earlier period, Period IV seems to have a greater concentration of baccalaureates continuing to the doctorate in humanities among the high-cost institutions.

TABLE 24. Average male index (college) in Period IV, by field and cost of attendance.

	31[a] $0-719	30 $720-805	30 $806-910	31 $911-1,039	32 $1,040-1,425
Foreign languages and literature	0.9[b]	0.9	0.9	0.5	1.9
History	2.1	2.0	2.3	1.8	3.5
English	1.6	1.5	1.6	1.8	4.1
Fine arts and music	0.2	0.4	0.3	0.5	0.7
Philosophy	0.5	1.4	0.6	0.4	1.6
TOTAL	5.2	6.2	5.8	5.1	11.7

[a] Number of institutions.
[b] Rate of Ph.D.'s per thousand baccalaureates.

But here, two observations should be made. First, it is entirely possible that the time interval between baccalaureate and doctorate degrees is significantly longer for graduates of lower-cost institutions than for those from higher-cost institutions. If this be so, then with the lapse of time one could expect that the lower-cost groups would gradually gain upon the high-cost group. On the other hand, students in Period IV have more economic and geographic mobility. Thousands of students matriculated in the postwar years under government subsidy, probably causing the concentration of high intellectual talent in relatively few and select institutions. In this recent period, motivation and ability, rather than money and propinquity, may have dictated college selection.

Table 25 relates Ph.D. production in the humanities to the type of administrative control, for the postwar period (Period IV) under consideration.

TABLE 25. Average male index in Period IV, by field and type of administrative control.

	30[a] Catholic	86 Protestant	38 Nondenominational
Foreign languages and literature	0.2[b]	1.2	1.7
History	1.0	2.2	4.1
English	1.4	1.9	3.8
Fine arts and music	0.04	0.4	0.8
Philosophy	0.6	0.7	1.5
TOTAL	3.3	6.4	11.9

[a] Number of institutions.
[b] Rate of Ph.D.'s per thousand baccalaureates.

The figures are entirely reminiscent of those of the third period. The nondenominational institutions stand comfortably ahead of the other two categories in all fields, whereas the Protestant institutions, on the average, appear to have declined. But recall that the liberal arts sample for this period includes a number of smaller Protestant institutions that were excluded from the earlier liberal arts sample because of size. The admission of this class of newly enlarged institutions may have served to depress the average attainment of this category. Catholic colleges, again, show the lowest average index.

Dividing this sample into men's and coeducational institutions as was done for the third period, we find that the average index of both is 7.1, suggesting that the earlier lag of coeducational institutions no longer exists. This is true in terms of over-all figures. However, if one breaks down these figures (as was done for Period III) into Catholic and non-Catholic, a more specific kind of picture results as is shown in Table 26.

TABLE 26. Average male index in Period IV,
by male and coeducational as well as
Catholic and Non-Catholic types.

Male vs. Coed Total		Male vs. Coed Total by Affiliation			
		Male Total		Coed Total	
52[a]	102	26	26	4	98
Male	Coed	Cath.	Non-Cath.	Cath.	Non-Cath.
7.1[b]	7.1	3.7	10.6	1.7	7.6

[a] Number of institutions.
[b] Rate of Ph.D.'s per thousand baccalaureates.

The results are now virtually identical with those obtained for our earlier sample, and it need only be repeated that non-Catholic men's institutions appear to be significantly most productive, whereas Catholic coeducational institutions are the least productive. Perhaps the most important distinction to be observed here, as before, is that between the Catholic and non-Catholic institutions, since the number of Catholic coeducational institutions is excessively small.

This chapter has examined some of the obvious variables affecting production of humanistic scholars. An agronomist might raise the same query concerning the characteristics of farms having high or low yields per acre as a function of their location, the amount invested in cultivation, and the type of proprietorship under which they were held. Three distinct variables all bear striking relation to the rate of scholarly production of humanists, and with remarkable consistency in the two historical periods examined.

It should be evident to the reader, however, that these three basic variables are by no means independent of each other. Cost is related to region, as well as to type of administrative control; type of administrative control is not independent of region or cost. It is especially in the northeastern part of the United States (notably New England), that high cost of attendance and nondenominational administrative control are associated with a high yield of humanistic scholars. This pattern is indeed entirely consistent with the findings reported in *The Younger American Scholar* (1953). Most of the younger humanistic scholars of distinction, at the period of this study, had not attained their doctorates, but had merely been awarded some graduate distinction, governmental, private, or otherwise. It is interesting to note that this pattern has not historically characterized the output of scientists. They showed, in contrast to the humanists, a radically different pattern of origins with respect to cost and region in the 1930's. In more recent times these differences remain in effect, but less incisively.

Some suggestive trends emerge from comparisons between Periods III and IV. We shall concern ourselves here only with the general humanities index. There is some evidence that the geographic gradient that placed New England in such marked eminence in Period III has more recently become somewhat reduced, particularly as the Midwest moves from an obscure to a promising position. We shall subsequently look at the position of the humanist at three typical midwestern universities. At that point I shall have occasion to advance the thesis that this region is becoming increasingly hospitable to the humanities, at least in its larger universities and hopefully in its smaller colleges.

A second observation is that the cost gradient has, if anything, become more, rather than less extreme in the most recent period. Thus, in recent times the most costly institutions have shown more striking superiority over others than in our prewar period. I am inclined to attribute this fact to the mobility of the American student in an age of prosperity and government subsidy; our ablest and most dedicated younger minds were able to select their undergraduate college with greater freedom and discernment than was possible in earlier periods.

With respect to the type of administrative control, there is small difference to be observed between the two periods. There is a remarkable consistency in both periods with respect to the average humanistic production of institutions classed according to Catholic and non-Catholic control, and male and coeducational student bodies.

❧ 5 ❧

A SAMPLE OF UNIVERSITIES

This chapter parallels Chapter 4 in general design and purpose. Here, however, we shall deal with a sample of universities from Periods III, and a sample from Period IV, including a great many of our public institutions. The liberal arts samples just reviewed were confined to private colleges. To be included in the university samples, my criterion was that an institution maintain, in the period concerned, a doctoral program in at least one of the fields of humanities. Analysis of these samples was made in terms of region, cost of attendance, and type of administrative control. Here, as in Chapter 4, we deal not with absolute numbers of humanistic scholars, but with the rate per thousand of graduates, that is, the humanistic index. It should be borne in mind that the averages are weighted, taking into account both size of institution and number of scholars.

Let us turn first to Period III. Table 27 presents the partial index

TABLE 27. Average male index (university) in Period III, by field and region.

	5[a] New England	15 Mid- Atlantic	9 South	19 Midwest	7 West
Foreign languages and literature	3.2[b]	1.2	1.0	1.0	1.3
History	4.4	1.8	2.1	1.8	3.1
English	4.2	1.8	2.0	1.7	1.8
Fine arts and music	1.2	0.5	0.3	0.7	0.3
Philosophy	1.1	1.1	0.2	0.6	0.5
TOTAL	14.1	6.4	5.6	5.9	6.5

[a] Number of institutions.
[b] Rate of Ph.D.'s per thousand baccalaureates.

for the five fields, together with the total index, for each of the five major geographic regions. Here we may observe results highly consistent with those obtained for the liberal arts sample of the same period. The rate for New England schools is much higher than for schools of other geographic regions; this differential, in fact, is more

49

striking among the universities than among the liberal arts colleges. The superiority of the New England universities, moreover, is consistently present in all five fields. Probably the only departure worthy of comment is the relatively high standing of western universities in history.

A second analysis is in terms of cost of attendance. Here again, as for the liberal arts colleges, I have obtained figures from *American Universities and Colleges* for the years 1936 and 1940, averaged them, and divided the institutions into five roughly equal categories. Table 28 shows the average partial and total indices for each

TABLE 28. Average male index (university) in
Period III, by field and cost of attendance.

	11[a] $0-369	11 $370-494	11 $495-624	11 $625-766	11 $767-1,087
Foreign languages and literature	0.8[b]	0.9	1.4	1.4	2.1
History	1.4	1.6	3.2	2.5	3.0
English	1.1	1.6	1.5	2.1	3.2
Fine arts and music	0.5	0.5	0.3	0.9	0.7
Philosophy	0.3	0.3	0.6	1.6	1.0
TOTAL	4.1	5.0	6.9	8.4	10.1

[a] Number of institutions.
[b] Rate of Ph.D.'s per thousand baccalaureates.

of these five cost groupings. Here there is an unusually consistent and accelerated rate of production of humanistic scholars as the cost increases; the most costly fifth is almost two and one half times as productive, on the average, as the least costly fifth. This gradient, moreover, holds with tolerable consistency throughout the entire table of partial indices. This result is also congruent with that of liberal arts institutions in this same period.

A third mode of analysis involves classification by type of administrative control—Catholic, Protestant, nondenominational, and public. Table 29 lists the average general index for each type, and the average partial indices. In this instance the Catholic institutions yield the highest index. Their position is largely due to the special emphasis given philosophy at Catholic universities, where their average partial index is almost five times that of any other group of institutions. On the other hand, we may note the Catholic universities' peculiar weak-

TABLE 29. Average male index (university) in
Period III, by field and type of administrative control.

	6[a] Catholic	2 Protestant	20 Non-denominational	27 Public
Foreign languages and literature	2.1[b]	1.1	1.8	0.9
History	3.1	2.5	3.0	1.8
English	2.8	2.3	2.8	1.4
Fine arts and music	0.0	2.0	0.8	0.5
Philosophy	4.3	0.9	0.9	0.3
TOTAL	12.3	8.8	9.3	4.9

[a] Number of institutions.
[b] Rate of Ph.D.'s per thousand baccalaureates.

ness in the fields of fine arts and music, in the face of clearly superior
performance in history, foreign languages, and English. Much the
same picture was seen in the liberal arts sample, where Catholic colleges were productive in philosophy and deficient in fine arts and
music. On the other hand, the high average rate of Catholic universities' production marks them off from the comparatively poor average
of Catholic liberal arts colleges. The relatively poor standing of publicly supported universities is manifest in all five fields of the humanities.

The six universities with all-male student bodies yield an average
total index of 15.3 compared with 5.8 for coeducational universities.
The Period IV trend again is consistent with that of liberal arts colleges.

The sample of universities in Period IV (1946-59) is slightly
greater than in Period III, reflecting postwar educational expansion
and the greater number of institutions granting Ph.D.'s. With these
thoughts in mind, we turn to consider the way in which geographical
region is related to production of humanists. Table 30 shows the
average partial index for the five regions, as well as the average general index. Here, as in Period III and as with the liberal arts sample,
New England institutions are the most productive—almost two and
one-half times more productive than the average institution in the
other four regions. This pre-eminence is held with almost monotonous
regularity throughout all five fields and deserves no further elabora-
tion.

TABLE 30. Average male index (university) in
Period IV, by field and region.

	7[a] New England	20 Mid-Atlantic	16 South	21 Midwest	10 West
Foreign languages and literature	3.0[b]	1.1	0.7	0.8	1.4
History	4.9	1.8	1.2	1.5	2.2
English	4.4	1.7	1.9	1.7	1.7
Fine arts and music	1.3	0.4	0.2	0.4	0.6
Philosophy	1.3	0.8	0.4	0.6	0.4
TOTAL	14.9	5.8	4.5	5.0	6.3

[a] Number of institutions.
[b] Rate of Ph.D.'s per thousand baccalaureates.

We shall turn next to cost of attendance. Once again I have divided
institutions into five groups, according to cost of attendance during
the period (determined by averaging two representative years). Table
31 presents the average partial and total indices for the five major
groups.

TABLE 31. Average male index (university) in
Period IV, by field and cost of attendance.

	16[a] $0-611	16 $612-724	15 $725-949	13 $950-1,129	14 $1,130-1,400
Foreign languages and literature	0.4[b]	1.2	0.6	0.8	2.2
History	0.8	1.8	1.2	1.8	3.7
English	1.2	1.8	1.1	1.8	3.5
Fine arts and music	0.2	0.5	0.2	0.8	0.9
Philosophy	0.2	0.5	0.3	1.1	1.4
TOTAL	2.9	5.7	3.4	6.3	11.8

[a] Number of institutions.
[b] Rate of Ph.D.'s per thousand baccalaureates.

The gradient here is very striking indeed: the topmost fifth yields almost 12 humanists per 1000, the lowest fifth only 3 per 1000. This
cost gradient is much more striking than that of Period III, and suggests that the better students have recently become more concentrated
in high-cost universities. In the preceding chapter I conjectured on the
causes of this same condition in liberal arts colleges; here we find confirmation of Chapter 4's evidence.

Finally, Table 32 presents the average partial and general indices for Catholic, Protestant, nondenominational, and public institutions.

TABLE 32. Average male index (university) in
Period IV, by field and type of administrative control.

	6[a]	4	26	37
			Non-	
	Catholic	Protestant	denominational	Public
Foreign languages				
and literature	0.6[b]	0.9	1.7	0.8
History	2.1	1.6	2.9	1.4
English	2.2	2.9	2.7	1.4
Fine arts and music	0.3	0.9	0.7	0.3
Philosophy	2.6	0.4	1.0	0.4
TOTAL	7.8	6.7	9.1	4.4

[a] Number of institutions.
[b] Rate of Ph.D.'s per thousand baccalaureates.

The average indices for all except the Catholic institutions are essentially the same as those reported for Period III. Catholic institutions do appear to drop in average rate from the third period, but one doubts that the drop is significant. Catholic institutions are, after all, small in number, and their interval between baccalaureate and doctorate fairly high. They retain a singular eminence in the field of philosophy whereas, once again, their position in the fine arts and music is negligible. I shall later discuss the general pattern of Catholic higher education and note that, to an unusual degree, Catholic graduate schools recruit students from Catholic undergraduate institutions. These Catholic universities' low production of baccalaureates who later receive the Ph.D. in fine arts and music may simply result from the curricular pattern of Catholic graduate instruction which offers far fewer doctorates in these fields than do public, nondenominational, and Protestant institutions.

Finally, it may be observed that the nine all-male universities yield 15.9 humanists per thousand, whereas the remaining institutions yield only 5.1, a result remarkably consistent with that of Period III's university sample.

In summary, both periods seem to provide similar pictures. Universities in New England and those of high cost prove to be very sharply separated from institutions in other regions and of lower cost. This differential extends across all five fields of the humanities and is entirely consistent with the study of the liberal arts sample in the preceding chapter. Again one notes the special superiority of universities and liberal arts colleges with exclusively male student bodies. Probably the only striking difference is the high standing of Catholic universities as compared with Catholic liberal arts colleges. In a later section of this book I shall have occasion to speak of Catholic education and the humanities, and to review one major Catholic university in some detail.

⊷ 6 ⊶

FURTHER REMARKS ON
BACCALAUREATE ORIGINS

This chapter will conclude the discussion of baccalaureate origins of humanistic scholars. Chapters 3 and 4 have presented lists of institutions with highest absolute yield and highest indices of productivity (rate per thousand of baccalaureates produced). Chapter 4 has analyzed these rates for two samples of liberal arts colleges, and Chapter 5 for two samples of universities. These analyses related rates of humanistic production in recent decades to such factors as geographic location, cost of attendance, type of administrative control, and character of student body. It remains to comment on the production of female scholars for these same periods.

The numbers involved here scarcely warrant proceeding in the same systematic fashion that characterized my treatment of male scholars; however, a list of institutions that produce the most female scholars is surely of interest. Table 33 shows such a list. For male indices I established a lower limit of ten scholars per thousand; here my lower limit is but five per thousand, since only four schools for Period III (1936-45) and two for Period IV (1946-59) exceed ten scholars per thousand. Only institutions with sixty or more graduates per year have been included. Virtually all of the institutions with high indices are small and none in either list is publicly supported. Prominent in both lists are the eastern women's colleges of high prestige, although there are several Catholic women's colleges in both lists. In both lists, coeducational institutions are in the minority. Interestingly, the number of institutions that meet the lower limit of 5 Ph.D.'s per 1,000 baccalaureates in Period III is twice that of Period IV; the same trend occurred with respect to male indices, and may be explained by one of two factors. First, the time lag between baccalaureate and doctorate is appreciably larger for women scholars than for men. Second, there recently may have been a greater concentration of scholarly material in high-cost, private women's colleges and a corresponding concentration of female Ph.D. candidates. In any event the list presented here clearly confirms the limited degree to

55

TABLE 33. Female indices of production (number of humanistic scholars per thousand baccalaureates) in Periods III and IV.

Period III

Bryn Mawr	30.2	Agnes Scott	8.0
Manhattanville	14.9	Fordham	7.5
Swarthmore	13.1	Immaculate Heart	6.6
Radcliffe	11.6	Carleton	6.5
Vassar	9.7	Wooster	5.6
Catholic U.	9.5	Siena Heights	5.6
Mount Holyoke	8.8	Chicago	5.4
Wilson	8.4	Wellesley	5.3
St. Joseph's (Brooklyn)	8.2	Trinity	5.1

Period IV

Swarthmore	23.6	San Francisco	7.4
Bryn Mawr	15.5	Vassar	6.9
Wellesley	8.7	Siena Heights	6.5
Radcliffe	8.1	Catholic U.	5.8
Barnard	7.7	Chicago	5.5

which women contribute to the humanistic disciplines; further, it points up the remarkably small number of schools that show a significant rate of scholarly production for women in the humanities.

In the ensuing sections of this chapter, I should like to address myself to some long-range trends of American undergraduate study. Beyond this I will set forth some data on the proportion of recent undergraduates who chose to major in the humanities.

Through the courtesy of the Woodrow Wilson Fellowship Foundation I have obtained a body of data partially drawn from an earlier source,[1] but extended to the year 1958. This data gives the percentage of baccalaureates and first professional degrees awarded in all accredited institutions in the United States by fields and in five-year periods from 1901 to 1955. Thereafter the chart gives the percentage for single years, 1956 through 1958.

The fields of concentration are divided into nine general categories. The humanities, by my system of classification, include English, foreign languages, philosophy, the fine and applied arts, and history, although the last in the original chart is classified as a social science. I have taken the liberty of reorganizing this data to conform to my classifica-

[1] Dael Wolfle, *America's Resources of Specialized Talent* (Harper, 1954).

tions. It is presented in Table 34 and shows the percentage of baccalaureate and first professional degrees by each of the nine general categories and for the five areas of humanistic scholarship that particularly concern us.

First, a comment on each of these five fields. The decline of English
as a field of concentration is remarkably consistent, falling off steadily
from a 7.5 per cent average before World War I to 4.5 per cent in
the most recent period. This phenomenon, of course, must be seen
against the tremendously increased enrollment in American education
generally. Nevertheless, in terms of percentage, far fewer undergraduates major in English today than in the past. In the case of languages,
the falling off is even more abrupt, largely, I suspect, because of the
sharp decline in the study of Latin and Greek from the Victorian age
to the present. Until World War I, languages claimed very nearly
12 per cent of all baccalaureates, whereas in the most recent decade
this figure barely exceeds one per cent. Thus undergraduate concentration in languages has suffered far more acutely than in English. However, since the number of college students has increased approximately
tenfold in the last fifty years, it would be difficult to say whether the
absolute number of persons concentrating in languages has actually
decreased. Philosophy has never held major attraction for undergraduates. All the same, it dropped from slightly less than 5 per cent in the
first decade of the century to less than one per cent from 1956 on-
ward. It has declined less than languages, but more than English.
History, however, presents a rather stable picture over a period of almost sixty years. If anything, there is a very slight rising trend in the
most recent years of record. Between 1900 and 1910 slightly under
3 per cent of all students in the United States majored in history; in
1957-58 the figure stood at 3.5 per cent. Thus history appears to have
maintained its proportional numbers, despite the rise of a variety of
other fields that were little studied before World War I. The trend in
the fine and applied arts seems fairly well defined. During the first
two decades of the twentieth century the figure averages less than
one per cent. Thereafter appears a fairly steady rise until the 1950's
and a slight suggestion of leveling off or even decline in the most recent period. Over-all, however, this field has increased fourfold
since the turn of the century.

Of these five humanistic fields, then, two, languages and philosophy,
show a very sharp drop in percentage since 1900; English shows a

TABLE 34. Bachelors' and first professional degrees awarded in the United States, 1901-57, by field (in per cent).

Field	1901-05	1906-10	1911-15	1916-20	1921-25	1926-30	1931-35	1936-40	1941-45	1946-50	1951-55	1955-56	1956-57	1957-58
Humanities	27.7	27.7	26.9	25.4	21.6	21.7	19.0	16.9	16.0	14.8	15.0	15.7	13.5	13.5
English	7.0	7.6	7.9	7.8	7.0	6.9	6.2	5.7	5.2	4.4	4.3	4.6	4.5	4.6
Languages	12.2	11.9	11.1	9.9	8.0	7.2	5.3	3.7	2.6	1.5	1.3	1.3	1.3	1.2
Philosophy	4.9	4.6	4.2	3.4	2.1	1.9	1.8	1.6	1.3	1.6	1.5	0.9	0.8	0.8
History	2.4	3.0	3.2	3.1	3.1	3.1	2.9	3.1	3.1	3.2	3.1	3.5	3.4	3.5
Arts (fine & applied)	1.2	0.6	0.5	1.2	1.4	2.6	2.8	2.8	3.8	4.1	4.8	5.4	3.5	3.4
Natural sciences	13.3	14.1	14.3	13.9	12.7	12.4	10.4	10.4	10.9	10.7	8.6	6.3	7.9	7.8
Social sciences	1.7	2.8	3.8	4.5	5.7	6.9	7.3	8.1	8.7	10.6	10.2	10.4	10.1	10.3
Engineering	3.3	4.3	6.0	9.3	10.3	7.0	8.8	7.6	8.8	11.3	8.9	8.5	9.2	9.7
Applied biology	0.2	0.4	2.0	6.7	5.1	3.9	4.2	5.6	6.5	5.3	5.3	4.8	3.0	2.7
Health fields	33.2	27.9	23.2	16.1	12.1	9.5	7.0	6.1	7.4	5.9	6.7	7.1	6.8	6.5
Business & commerce	0.2	0.4	0.7	2.2	5.8	5.6	6.9	8.8	8.6	14.6	14.3	15.2	13.7	14.0
Education	0.4	0.2	1.3	3.1	7.5	14.0	20.1	23.1	22.4	14.8	19.3	18.5	22.8	22.7
Other fields[1]	20.0	22.2	21.8	18.8	19.2	19.0	17.1	13.4	10.7	12.0	11.7	13.5	13.0	12.8
	100.0	100.0	100.0	100.0	100.0	100.0	100.0	100.0	100.0	100.0	100.0	100.0	100.0	100.0

[1] Includes law, architecture, journalism, library science, and social work.
SOURCES: For years 1901-53, Dael Wolfle, *America's Resources of Specialized Talent* (Harper, 1954); for years 1954-57, U.S. Department of Health, Education, and Welfare, Office of Education, *Earned Degrees Conferred by Higher Educational Institutions*, Circulars #418, 461, 499, and 527.

substantial although not catastrophic decline; history holds its own very well indeed, with possibly a slight upward trend; only in the fine and applied arts is there a clear and manifest percentage increase. The development of new curricular offerings in the last field may be the main reason for increased enrollment. Moreover, the percentages involved at the beginning of the century are very small. It may further be observed that concentration in the fine and applied arts as classified here may not constitute probable basis for a career in humanistic scholarship. I have presented evidence to indicate that, in the main, the effective recruitment of scholars in music and the arts is not accomplished in departments that emphasize composition and performance. Rather, these scholars emerge from a small number of institutions whose emphasis is strongly directed toward historical scholarship. Although some may take heart in this seemingly rising trend in the fine arts, I consider it of dubious importance and probably deceptive with regard to the main concern of this study.

The plain fact is that the humanities have lost ground over the past six decades as far as the proportion of students concentrating at the baccalaureate level. This picture may be less discouraging than might appear at first sight. We must recall that the range of offerings provided at the collegiate level, particularly in applied fields, has greatly expanded. At the same time, the publicly supported higher educational system of America, less hospitable to the humanities than the privately supported system, has burgeoned.

It might be enlightening to see how other areas have fared. I shall not present the figures here for each of the disciplines in the remaining eight classifications shown in Table 34; it is sufficient to consider the over-all figures. The natural sciences have shown a rate of decline from the first to the sixth decade of approximately the same order as the field of English, moving from a little below 14 per cent in the first decade to a little over 7 per cent in the recent period. The social sciences, on the other hand, from which I have eliminated the field of history, show a dramatically ascending pattern. From a little over 2 per cent in the first decade to over 10 per cent in the sixth decade, the figure rises more or less evenly and continuously, showing that social sciences have been conspicuous gainers in their claims upon the American baccalaureate population. Engineering has shown a reasonably even upward progression, from approximately 4 per cent to 9 per cent, whereas applied biology (including home economics) moves from a minute fraction to approximately 3 per cent. The health fields, so-called, are conspicuous losers, especially the professional fields of medicine and dentistry, which have been reduced fivefold in six decades. By all odds the two most burgeoning areas are education and business and commerce. These were scarcely recognized areas for baccalaureate concentration in the first decade of our century whereas in most recent decades they account for over 35 per cent of all baccalaureates granted. Education alone accounted for about 23 per cent of all baccalaureates given in the most recent period. The "other fields"—law, architecture, journalism, library science, and social work—show a decline from approximately 20 per cent in the first decade to a little over 13 per cent in the sixth, roughly paralleling the decline of the humanities and the natural sciences.

The picture to be gleaned from these figures is remarkably lucid. As the American system of higher education has vastly expanded its enrollment over the last six decades, it has done so particularly by providing utilitarian, technical, and vocational avenues to the baccalaureate degree. As a result, a lesser percentage of college students are attracted to the humanities. Furthermore, this expansion of enrollment has been far more conspicuous in public coeducational institutions. I shall present evidence to indicate that in coeducational schools the majority of humanistic baccalaureates are usually women. This may be a matter of social coercion and custom, or possibly because these disciplines are so often used as avenues to primary and secondary school teaching. In any event, the fact suggests that the percentage decline in the humanities, including both sexes, may actually understate the threat to these disciplines, for there are good grounds for believing that the proportion of women concentrating in these disciplines has increased with the rise of public coeducational institutions in America. Very few of these women continue their study to a Ph.D., as noted earlier.

The disposition of various student bodies to elect different fields of concentration is worth examination. No final decision shall be made here whether the propensity to study humanities in a particular institution is determined by its student clientele or by the drawing power of certain departments or faculty members. Surely both factors are involved in some degree. We have, however, already seen suggestive evidence attaching high importance to the regional and socio-economic background from which a student body is drawn. At this juncture I would surmise that the attraction to the humanities is particularly associated with eastern urban background, higher socio-economic status, and a general tradition favoring intellectual, as opposed to utilitarian, values as educational objectives.

I should like to be able to offer definitive and exact data on the distribution of majors in the different types of institutions—obviously, one factor determining productivity in the humanities is the percentage of undergraduate students who concentrate in them. Unfortunately, I must admit some embarrassment in attempting any definitive analysis. It must be plainly stated that the statistical source upon which I depend is in several respects difficult to evaluate. Nevertheless, I shall attempt to glean from this source certain statistics presenting a high degree of congruence, and thereby confirm what thoughtful opinion would suggest. Accordingly I have selected three groups of institutions for comparison. The first of these consists of the nineteen state universities that appear among the most productive institutions as shown in Table 9 in Chapter 3. The second group is composed of the nine eastern Ivy League men's institutions, all of which again appear among the high producers in Table 9. Six eastern women's colleges notable for their high yield of female scholars in the humanities make up the third group. The percentage of each school's students who majored in the humanities, and the percentage in the sciences, in the year 1957-58, were determined. A special qualification should be added here: I was forced to determine these percentages by approximation, using graduate figures for the year 1953-54 because of the statistical corruption in the figures available through the federal source for 1957-58. All the same, it is probably fair to say that the percentages reported are approximately correct, and indeed, as we shall see, the differences between the three groups of institutions are so striking that it undoubtedly overrides any imprecision in the figures.

Table 35 lists the three groups of institutions, together with the percentage of students majoring in the humanities and those in the sciences for the year 1957-58. A further division into male and female has been made for coeducational institutions. The percentage list of those concentrating in the humanistic fields shows a very clear progression. Men in all but six state universities elected the humanities less than 10 per cent of the time, and in only two instances does the figure exceed 20 per cent. Here, too, the percentage of women concentrating in the humanities is consistently higher than the percentage of men.

TABLE 35. Estimated percentages of undergraduates majoring in the humanities and sciences in 1957-58 for coed state universities, eastern men's colleges and eastern women's colleges.

Institution	Per cent Humanities		Per cent Sciences	
	Male	Female	Male	Female
Cornell	5.5	16.4	10.7	7.2
Indiana	4.4	15.3	8.5	2.2
Michigan State	6.4	14.5	6.9	5.0
State U. of Ohio	6.0	10.9	8.5	2.9
Rutgers	8.7	36.8	4.0	14.2
State U. of Iowa	9.6	28.4	5.1	2.3
California (all campuses)	10.6	29.6	13.4	5.2
Colorado	5.7	17.3	4.7	2.7
Illinois	4.3	19.7	6.9	7.0
Kansas	8.0	18.3	11.2	7.7
Michigan	13.1	28.3	9.2	6.4
Minnesota (all campuses)	9.5	13.9	7.2	2.6
New Mexico	10.9	24.3	12.3	8.8
North Carolina	22.6	32.6	9.6	5.7
Texas	10.3	38.2	14.5	9.1
Utah	9.5	13.8	8.6	1.1
Virginia	25.9	a	9.9	a
Washington	8.2	15.4	7.6	3.6
Wisconsin	9.3	25.5	8.3	3.8
Amherst	30.5	—	28.3	—
Dartmouth	39.1	—	8.2	—
Harvard	37.1	—	20.6	—
Haverford	36.0	—	18.9	—
Princeton	37.6	—	14.8	—
Trinity	39.6	—	5.7	—
Wesleyan	39.5	—	30.8	—
Williams	46.8	—	23.4	—
Yale	31.0	b	5.2	—
Bryn Mawr	—	59.2	—	21.6
Mount Holyoke	—	38.6	—	14.4
Radcliffe	—	58.7	—	11.7
Smith	—	68.0	—	9.0
Vassar	—	50.9	—	8.5
Wellesley	—	63.6	—	18.3

a Figures for female majors inaccurate or unavailable.
b Thirteen women were listed as undergraduate majors at Yale but since this is an all-male institution the figure was considered inaccurate.

Clearly, in this sample of the state universities, the humanities universally attract a higher percentage of women than men. The eastern Ivy League institutions, with their all-male constituencies, have percentages in the humanities ranging from 30 per cent upward. Their student bodies are much more prone to concentrate in the humanities than are the male populations of state universities; for that matter, Ivy League men study the humanities more often than women of state universities. Finally, it may be observed that among high-cost and highly productive eastern women's colleges the percentage of students concentrating in the humanities exceeds the men's Ivy League institutions, and averages in excess of 50 per cent.

In summary, therefore, it is clear that both sex of student and type of institution are very significantly correlated with the disposition to concentrate in humanistic studies. Men in state universities are least disposed, next come women in state universities and then men in Ivy League institutions; most disposed of all to major in the humanities are the women in prestigious eastern women's institutions. This order, when sex is taken into account, corresponds roughly to the average indices of humanistic scholarly production for the three types of institutions.

Let us now consider the percentages that have been determined for those concentrating in the sciences. Here it will be observed that in the state universities there is no particular tendency for men to elect the sciences more frequently than the humanities. On the other hand, in all but one instance in the state universities we find the percentage of women concentrating in science to be substantially less than the percentage concentrating in humanities. Thus, in the large coeducational state institutions the humanities tend to be the province of the female sex and the sciences of the male sex. Turning to the men's Ivy League sample, we immediately note that the percentage concentrating in the sciences is consistently less than the percentage concentrating in the humanities, a pattern similar to that obtained for women in state universities. But we should also note that the percentages here are in the main very much higher than those for men in state universities, a condition arising from the lack of practical and vocational fields of concentration in Ivy League institutions. Finally, it should be observed that the percentage of women concentrating in the sciences in our Ivy League women's colleges is conspicuously less than in the humanities, presenting a vivid contrast. At the same time, however, we should note that this percentage is on the average far higher than for women in any of our state institutions, or, for that matter, higher on the average than for men in state institutions.

What does all this amount to? In the first place it is clear that, compared with our eastern Ivy League institutions, whether male or female, the state universities are attracting a relatively small percentage of their students to either the sciences or the humanities as I have described them. This should not be too surprising, since we know that the pattern of these publicly supported institutions leans heavily to service and utilitarian objectives and offers majors in such subjects as home economics, business administration, and physical education that are not offered in our eastern private institutions. Thus the first rule is that both the sciences and the humanities in the state universities attract small percentages of students. Beyond this, however, is the very important matter of the appeal of humanities and sciences to the two sexes. It seems quite clearly demonstrated, if the above data may be trusted, that the humanities tend to be elected by the female sex, whereas the sciences are conceived as the masculine domain; this proposition is clearly sustained whether we consider Ivy League institutions, male and female, or the election of the sexes within coeducational state institutions. We therefore emerge with what might be described as a two-factor theory of the forces determining attraction of the humanities. The first is related to the type and climate of the institution itself—e.g., eastern Ivy League institutions appear to be hospitable to, and foster the study of, the humanities, whereas state universities provide a less hospitable climate. The second factor is related to the sex of the student and clearly suggests that the humanities are proportionately more frequently selected by females than males as areas of concentration, while the converse holds for the natural sciences.

The major sections of this study have so far dealt with doctorates in the humanities without making any attempt to recognize differences in quality. For scientists, it is always possible to take account of such special distinction as membership in the National Academy of Sciences or "starred" status in *American Men of Science*. For scholars of the humanities, there is no such ready means of identification of high distinction. It proved possible, however, to obtain from the American Council of Learned Societies a listing of those persons granted fellowships and grants-in-aid for the years 1958 through 1962. These persons were selected to receive special distinction by an impartial panel of their

64

peers and may be regarded as a particularly distinguished body of scholars in the humanities. It is of some interest to examine the doctoral and baccalaureate origins of this group. Of the 445 scholars falling within this category, information concerning their origins was obtained from 397, who constitute the sample under consideration. The distribution of these scholars by year and by field is shown in Table 36, where it will be observed that while a small number of awards was granted outside our five areas of scholarship, the overwhelming majority fell within them, with the greatest number in the field of English.

TABLE 36. Distribution of American Council of Learned Societies awardees 1958-62 by field of specialization.

	1958-59	1959-60	1960-61	1961-62	Total
Foreign languages	20	23	22	20	85
History	12	15	36	18	81
English	25	18	30	40	123
Fine arts & music	17	18	22	16	73
Philosophy	8	6	11	8	33
Anthropology	1	—	—	1	2
Sociology	—	—	2	1	3
History of science	—	—	1	1	2
Philosophy of science	—	—	1	—	1
Religion	—	1	2	1	4
TOTAL	83	81	127	106	397

Let us first examine the baccalaureate origins of this group of scholars. Table 37 lists all institutions that may be credited with three or more awardees. They have been divided into four groupings, according to the year of their baccalaureate degree. The total column is of most significance. We observe that 51 scholars are graduates of foreign institutions. Thereafter come Harvard, Princeton, Columbia, and Yale with totals of 32, 14, 14, and 11, respectively. Below this is a strong concentration of distinguished smaller colleges such as Oberlin, Wesleyan, and Dartmouth, and interspersed among them some of our larger and most famous state universities, such as California, Wisconsin, and Michigan.

The concentration of these awards, however, in Ivy League colleges and universities is even more striking than the data presented on the baccalaureate origins of Ph.D.'s in general. It seems quite clear that the

TABLE 37. Baccalaureate origins of ACLS awardees,
by period of baccalaureate degree.

Institution	I 1925	II 1926-35	III 1936-45	IV 1946-59	Total
Foreign universities	9	7	24	11	51
Harvard	3	4	11	14	32
Princeton	3	5	4	2	14
Columbia	—	1	4	9	14
Yale	2	2	3	4	11
Oberlin	2	2	2	3	9
NYU	—	3	3	2	8
California (Berkeley)	—	1	2	5	8
CCNY	1	2	1	3	7
Wesleyan	1	—	3	2	6
Chicago	1	1	3	1	6
Cornell	1	—	3	2	6
Wisconsin	—	2	2	2	6
Michigan	—	3	1	2	6
Dartmouth	1	—	2	2	5
Syracuse	1	2	2	—	5
Illinois	—	2	1	1	4
Western Reserve	—	3	—	1	4
UCLA	—	—	1	3	4
Davidson	1	1	1	1	4
Brown	1	—	1	2	4
Wabash	1	1	1	—	3
Northwestern	—	1	—	2	3
New Mexico	—	—	3	—	3
Rutgers	—	1	—	2	3
Baker	3	—	—	—	3
Swarthmore	—	—	—	3	3
Arizona	—	2	—	1	3
Ohio State	1	—	1	1	3
Williams	—	1	2	—	3
Institutions having 2 or 1 B.A.'s					122
No degree or no B.A. shown					34
TOTAL					397

consideration of this distinguished group of scholars in the humanities
merely shows a greater exaggeration of trends already observed elsewhere, indicating the special affinity of the humanities for private,
eastern universities and colleges.

7

DOCTORAL ORIGINS

Preceding chapters have dealt with the baccalaureate origins of individuals taking the doctorate in the humanities. This chapter will deal with the origins of the doctorate itself, that is, the schools at which American humanistic scholars receive their doctorates. Three sources provide data. The first of these is information prepared for me by the National Academy of Sciences, showing the B.A. origins from which successful doctoral candidates have been recruited since World War II in the thirty universities that produced most humanistic doctorates. These data reveal the region and type of institutions from which graduate schools draw their students, the proportion of their own baccalaureates that they accept, and the number in each humanistic field who were granted doctorates. Included in these statistics are persons who have taken a humanistic doctorate from these thirty universities through 1959 and who received that B.A. not earlier than 1946.

A second source of data is statistics prepared for me, again by the National Academy of Sciences, revealing the time interval between baccalaureate and doctorate degree at different major universities for each field of humanistic study, and for both men and women. These data are derived from the unusually detailed record of persons receiving doctorates in the humanities between 1957 and 1959. The third source of data is a publication of the National Academy of Sciences, *Doctorate Production in United States Universities 1936-56,* reporting the number of doctoral degrees granted by all institutions in all fields of scholarship.

Using these figures, we shall examine the thirty American universities that, in the period 1936-56, granted the greatest number of doctorates in our five humanistic fields. In this compilation, however, I have included only persons receiving a baccalaureate degree in the year 1946 or thereafter and claiming a doctorate by 1959 from one of these larger institutions.

Table 38 shows the number of such persons by institution, field, and sex; the table is presented here without any extensive comment. It does illustrate dramatically the degree to which a few graduate schools tend to be overwhelming in importance, both in particular fields and in the production of humanistic Ph.D.'s generally. Thus, the first five in order for male humanists are Harvard with 337, Yale with 279, Columbia with 240, Wisconsin with 211, and University of California at Berkeley with 160. The fact that the first three are Ivy League institutions is again to be remarked. Respecting differences in fields, one observes here again the relatively high standing of Catholic institutions in philosophy. And it is interesting to note a substantial difference in pattern between the leading contenders, Harvard and Yale. Harvard is notable for its number of Ph.D.'s in history, Yale for its doctorates in philosophy and English.

TABLE 38. Number of Ph.D.'s awarded to baccalaureates of the years 1946-59, by graduate school.

Graduate Institution	Sex	Field					
		Foreign Lang.	History	English	Fine Arts & Music	Philosophy	Total
Harvard	M	51	126	97	28	35	337
	F	1	0	0	0	0	1
Yale	M	77	55	80	14	53	279
	F	9	3	8	5	2	27
Columbia	M	43	86	55	6	50	240
	F	20	9	8	0	2	39
Wisconsin	M	35	98	66	3	9	211
	F	3	6	9	1	0	19
California (Berkeley)	M	50	66	37	2	14	169
	F	4	5	3	1	1	14
Pennsylvania	M	24	50	63	4	9	150
	F	4	2	2	1	0	9
Princeton	M	52	31	35	7	15	140
	F	0	0	0	0	0	0
Chicago	M	25	46	32	8	19	130
	F	1	3	2	2	0	8
Michigan	M	23	42	35	18	10	128
	F	1	2	4	2	1	10
State U. of Iowa	M	12	18	36	47	11	124
	F	3	0	0	2	0	5
Illinois	M	15	38	43	6	7	109
	F	6	1	3	0	0	10
Indiana	M	16	30	32	32	5	104
	F	2	1	2	1	1	7
North Carolina	M	35	29	23	5	2	94
	F	8	0	1	0	0	9

TABLE 38.

Graduate Institution	Sex	Foreign Lang.	History	English	Fine Arts & Music	Philosophy	Total
Stanford	M	8	36	34	2	2	82
	F	1	4	5	1	0	11
Northwestern	M	7	24	37	13	6	87
	F	3	1	1	0	0	5
Minnesota	M	3	37	30	3	7	80
	F	1	2	4	0	0	7
Texas	M	13	33	28	0	7	81
	F	2	2	2	0	0	6
Johns Hopkins	M	24	22	22	0	13	81
	F	4	0	0	0	0	4
Cornell	M	8	20	19	3	13	63
	F	4	3	3	0	0	10
Ohio State	M	2	20	22	18	4	66
	F	0	0	3	2	0	5
UCLA	M	8	26	13	5	10	62
	F	5	1	2	1	0	9
NYU	M	7	19	26	8	3	63
	F	1	1	1	1	2	6
Catholic U.	M	5	3	4	2	29	43
	F	5	8	1	1	6	21
Washington	M	11	11	20	0	6	48
	F	1	1	1	0	1	4
USC	M	10	17	6	11	3	47
	F	1	0	0	0	3	4
Duke	M	0	26	15	0	5	46
	F	0	1	1	0	1	3
Boston	M	3	15	7	11	8	44
	F	0	1	1	1	0	3
Vanderbilt	M	0	18	24	0	0	42
	F	0	1	3	0	0	4
Radcliffe	M	0	0	0	0	0	0
	F	11	16	7	5	4	43
Fordham	M	2	8	3	0	18	31
	F	1	0	1	0	1	3

The reader is invited to explore further particular comparisons. In passing, one should also note the characteristic paucity of women doctorates, who constitute only 8.8 per cent of the total under consideration.

Table 39 shows the percentage of persons within the sample who receive doctorates in different fields, by five geographic regions of the nation; figures for male and female scholars are henceforth combined.

TABLE 39. Production of Ph.D.'s in different humanistic fields, by geographic region.

	Foreign Lang.	History	English	Fine Arts & Music	Philosophy	Total
Northeast (4)						
No. Ph.D.'s	152	216	200	64	102	734
Per cent	20.7	29.4	27.2	8.7	13.9	
Mid-Atlantic (6)						
No. Ph.D.'s	166	229	215	30	113	754
Per cent	22.0	30.4	28.5	4.0	15.0	
South (6)						
No. Ph.D.'s	96	143	124	8	63	434
Per cent	22.1	32.9	28.6	1.8	14.5	
Midwest (9)						
No. Ph.D.'s	158	369	361	147	80	1,115
Per cent	14.2	33.1	32.4	13.2	7.2	
West (5)						
No. Ph.D.'s	92	168	122	23	37	442
Per cent	20.8	38.0	27.6	5.2	8.4	

This table deserves a few comments. We may note, for example, that the field of foreign languages and literature is probably significantly weak in the Midwest, a possible reflection of the isolationism of the area. In any event, all other regions exceed 20 per cent, whereas the Midwest shows but 14 per cent. History shows a fairly consistent percentage, but with some clear evidence of a rising trend as one moves westward. This confirms other indications that history, of the five humanistic fields, is the one that commands the most consideration among "grass-roots" institutions. The percentage in arts and music shows wide variation from region to region. It is notably small in southern universities, and especially high in the Midwest; however, consideration of the preceding table will show that, in good part, the figure for the Midwest is dependent upon the exceptional number of Ph.D.'s granted at the State University of Iowa, accounting for a third of the total. The doctorates granted here, moreover, are largely for composition and performance, in contrast to the eastern Ivy League doctorates in the arts, which are exclusively directed toward historical criticism. Finally, philosophy claims comparatively few in the Midwest and the West, and it shows notable concentration in the New England and Mid-

Atlantic regions. The South yields a high percentage of Ph.D.'s in philosophy but almost two-thirds of these are granted by a single institution, Catholic University of America in Washington, D.C. Thus, the homeland of philosophy would appear to be the Mid-Atlantic and New England states.

Table 40 shows the origin of Ph.D.'s within the sample classified by public, private, or Catholic institutions.

TABLE 40. Type of graduate school granting recent Ph.D.'s in the humanities.

	Foreign Lang.	History	English	Fine Arts & Music	Philosophy	Total
Public (13)						
No. Ph.D.'s	264	493	442	141	106	1,446
Per cent	18.2	34.1	30.6	9.7	7.3	
Private (15)						
No. Ph.D.'s	387	613	644	128	235	2,007
Per cent	19.3	30.5	32.1	6.4	11.7	
Catholic (2)						
No. Ph.D.'s	13	19	9	3	54	98
Per cent	13.3	19.4	9.2	3.1	55.1	

A comparison of public and private institutions shows no striking contrast in the percentages involved, except perhaps in the fact that private universities grant somewhat fewer doctorates than do public universities in the fields of fine arts and history and suggestively more in the field of philosophy. It is highly interesting to observe the radically variant pattern obtaining in Catholic universities. Here we find more than half of the humanistic degrees bestowed in the field of philosophy and a correspondingly small percentage in the other four areas.

Perhaps the most significant analysis of this body of data reveals the origins from which each of these universities has recruited its students. As a general rule there is a kind of provincialism that governs the recruitment of graduate students in the humanities. Graduate departments tend to recruit their students from undergraduate institutions lying within the same regions as the university and controlled by the same type of administration. Also, to a surprising degree, many of these universities recruit their own undergraduates for graduate study.

Table 41 shows the regional origins, by percentage, from which each of these thirty institutions has recruited its humanistic doctoral candidates since 1946. Note the striking degree to which, for virtually all types of institutions, the undergraduate origins of Ph.D.'s in the humanities are to be found in the geographic region of the university. Thus, for example, 62 per cent of the graduate students at Boston University come from New England. The figure stands at 51 per cent for Harvard and 42 per cent for Yale. The same tendency to localism will be found throughout all other regions and holds for both publicly and privately supported institutions.

A surprising degree of geographic immobility emerges from this table, considering the prosperity of the times and the character of contemporary graduate instruction. Unfortunately, a comparative figure for scientists could not be obtained. All the same, it seems most unlikely that such a geographical concentration would exist among the sciences in view of prior experience.[1]

What types of institutions have supplied humanities graduate students to the major universities since World War II? I have grouped these baccalaureate institutions under four headings, namely, public, nondenominational, Protestant and Jewish, and Catholic; I have computed, in addition, a figure called "per cent of *own product*," which describes the proportion of the Ph.D.'s in a university that has taken the baccalaureate at the same university. Thus Table 42 shows an impressive tendency, during the years 1946-59, for publicly supported universities to draw their graduate students from institutions of the same type. Private universities draw very heavily from nondenominational and Protestant undergraduate sources. Harvard and Yale, our two most productive institutions, take only 18 and 20 per cent, respectively, of their graduate students from public institutions, while 28 and 27 per cent, respectively, are their own baccalaureates. Beyond this, we may note that Harvard takes 71 per cent and Yale 65 per cent of its graduate students from nondenominational private universities and colleges, including their own undergraduate institutions.

On the other hand, examining our two most productive state universities, Berkeley and Wisconsin, we find that Berkeley draws 67 per cent and Wisconsin 48 per cent from public institutions; of their own

---

[1] Reported in Robert H. Knapp and H. B. Goodrich, *The Origins of American Scientists* (U. of Chicago, 1953) and in Robert H. Knapp, H. B. Goodrich, and G. A. W. Boehm, "The Origins of U.S. Scientists," *Scientific American,* CLXXXI, 1 (1951), 15-17.

TABLE 41. Region of baccalaureate institutions attended by Ph.D.'s.

| Institution | Origins in Per cent | | | | |
	New England	Mid-Atlantic	South	Midwest	West
New England					
Boston	61.7	8.5	10.7	12.7	6.4
Harvard	50.9	19.8	6.5	15.1	7.7
Radcliffe	53.5	27.9	2.3	14.0	2.3
Yale	42.5	27.1	7.1	15.0	8.1
Mid-Atlantic					
Columbia	12.9	59.9	7.9	12.2	7.2
Cornell	9.6	43.8	9.6	24.7	12.3
Fordham	20.6	61.8	5.9	11.7	0.0
New York	2.9	82.6	8.7	3.0	2.9
Princeton	15.7	45.0	12.9	17.8	8.5
Pennsylvania	8.2	63.5	14.5	8.8	5.0
South					
Catholic U.	7.8	10.9	57.9	18.7	3.2
Duke	6.1	14.3	57.1	18.3	4.0
Johns Hopkins	15.3	20.0	34.9	22.3	9.4
North Carolina	9.7	6.8	71.8	9.7	2.0
Vanderbilt	2.2	2.2	89.2	6.5	0.0
Texas	1.1	1.1	82.7	10.3	4.6
Midwest					
Indiana	9.0	10.8	15.0	55.0	9.9
Northwestern	5.4	12.0	18.4	62.0	2.2
Ohio State	5.7	18.3	12.7	54.9	8.5
State U. of Iowa	7.0	5.4	14.0	62.8	10.9
Chicago	6.5	10.1	7.9	67.4	7.9
Illinois	5.0	15.1	13.5	60.5	5.9
Michigan	11.6	8.0	7.3	65.2	8.0
Minnesota	6.9	4.6	13.8	63.2	11.5
Wisconsin	11.3	22.2	8.6	50.4	7.3
West					
Stanford	5.4	10.8	6.5	23.7	53.7
California (Berkeley)	6.3	9.1	7.5	10.3	66.9
UCLA	4.2	8.4	4.2	12.7	70.4
USC	3.9	5.9	7.8	11.7	70.5
Washington	7.7	7.7	3.8	19.2	61.6

TABLE 42. Type of institution at which Ph.D.'s prepared.

		Origins in Per cent			
Institution	Public	Non-Denomin.	Protestant	Catholic	Own Product
Public					
Cornell	34.3	49.3	12.3	4.1	13.7
Indiana	53.2	26.1	20.7	0.0	18.0
Ohio State	45.1	28.2	21.1	5.6	18.3
State U. of Iowa	58.1	13.2	25.6	3.1	22.5
California (Berkeley)	66.9	22.3	6.3	4.0	44.6
UCLA	67.6	16.9	14.1	1.4	50.7
Illinois	55.5	26.9	12.6	5.0	19.3
Michigan	55.1	23.9	15.2	5.8	26.1
Minnesota	52.9	19.5	25.3	2.3	20.7
North Carolina	46.6	16.5	35.0	1.9	19.4
Texas	62.1	8.0	27.6	2.3	27.6
Washington	53.9	25.0	17.3	3.8	38.5
Wisconsin	47.8	30.4	14.3	7.0	18.3
Private					
Boston U.	14.9	48.9	29.8	6.4	12.8
Columbia	34.8	55.6	8.2	1.4	18.3
Duke	18.4	22.4	57.1	2.0	10.2
Harvard	17.5	70.7	8.0	3.8	28.7
Johns Hopkins	20.0	51.8	24.7	3.5	18.8
NYU	40.6	47.9	2.9	8.7	29.0
Northwestern	23.9	26.1	42.4	7.6	26.1
Princeton	24.3	57.9	16.4	1.4	21.4
Radcliffe	14.0	74.4	4.7	7.0	16.3
Stanford	34.4	41.9	15.1	8.6	20.4
Chicago	22.5	63.8	9.4	4.3	43.4
Pennsylvania	23.3	51.6	19.5	5.7	23.9
USC	39.2	37.3	17.6	5.9	31.4
Vanderbilt	34.8	26.1	37.0	2.2	13.0
Yale	20.3	65.4	12.4	2.0	26.8
Catholic					
Catholic U.	1.6	6.2	3.1	85.9	34.4
Fordham	2.9	5.9	0.0	91.2	29.4

graduates, these schools take 45 and 18 per cent, respectively. Berkeley takes but 22 per cent of its graduate students from nondenominational private institutions, whereas Wisconsin takes only 30 per cent. The two most eminent Catholic universities represented, Catholic University and Fordham, show extraordinarily sharp concentration: 85 and 91 per cent, respectively, of their graduate students obtained their baccalaureates at Catholic institutions, whereas 35 and 29 per cent, respectively, are their own baccalaureates.

Table 42 leads one immediately to the recognition of three relatively clear and decisive pathways to the doctoral degree in humanities in America: the nondenominational-Protestant, the public, and the Catholic systems of colleges and universities. The third pathway is clearly the most constrained and involves the least interfusion with the other two. We have seen the overwhelming degree to which our foremost Catholic universities recruit their graduate students from the ranks of Catholic baccalaureates. State universities, as opposed to private colleges and universities, maintain a degree of separation that probably can be only partly explained by geographic considerations. Thus Stanford, to take a critical instance, takes 57 per cent of its graduate students from nondenominational and Protestant institutions and only 34 per cent from public institutions, despite the fact that it is located in a region dominated by great and powerful state universities. In contrast, Berkeley, but a few miles distant, takes 29 per cent from nondenominational and Protestant sources in contrast to 67 per cent from public sources. The differences between these institutions are explored in more detail in Chapter 12. In plain fact, one looks in vain for a single university approximating a balanced nationwide selection of its graduate students and even distribution of selection across the different classes of baccalaureate institutions. Even the most distinguished graduate institutions are restricted in their pattern of recruitment, showing marked regionalism and partisanship to institutions of their own type. The implications of this "three-channel" pattern cannot be fully discussed at this juncture, but Chapters 10-12 are devoted to examining the position of the humanities in two Ivy League universities, in several great state universities, and in one major Catholic university. There, among other things, I attempt to discuss the degree to which these three separate channels support different intellectual climates, outlooks, and emphases in their support of the humanities.

As reported earlier, the National Academy of Sciences has provided some interesting data that bear upon the rate of progress from the baccalaureate to the doctoral degree. The data concerning this "lag time" are based upon records obtained from recipients of doctorates at all universities and in all fields for the years 1957-59. The figures describing the lag time for the sciences have been presented in a publication,

The Science Doctorates of 1958 and 1959, by Lindsey R. Harmon and Herbert Soldz of the National Academy of Sciences. Figures describing the lag time for other fields have been obtained by me from the National Academy of Sciences. The humanities in general show greater lag time between the baccalaureate and the doctoral degree, whereas the sciences generally show the most rapid progression. Table 43 gives the median time intervals.

TABLE 43. Median lag time by field.

	Lag Time (years)
Chemistry	6.5
Physics	7.5
Biochemistry	7.7
Mathematics	8.1
Botany and phytopathology	8.2
Engineering	8.3
Agriculture and related fields	8.4
Microbiology	8.5
Genetics	8.5
Geology	8.6
Physiology and related fields	8.6
Zoology	9.0
Miscellaneous life sciences	9.0
Psychology	9.3
Medical sciences	9.3
Philosophy	9.4
Anthropology and archaeology	9.4
Economics	9.5
Geography	9.6
Speech	9.8
Political science	9.8
Sociology	9.9
History and civilization	9.9
Foreign languages and literature	10.0
English language and literature	10.3
Jurisprudence	10.3
Business and commerce	10.6
Fine arts and architecture	10.6
Miscellaneous	11.3
Education	12.5

The lag time has been obtained for the same thirty institutions discussed earlier in this chapter. Table 44 presents the mean lag time for these institutions for both male and female doctoral candidates.

TABLE 44. Average lag time, in years by graduate institution.

	Male	Female
Princeton	8.0	—
Johns Hopkins	8.1	14.0
Yale	8.4	8.2
Wisconsin	9.3	13.3
Duke	9.5	18.0
Harvard	9.7	—
Cornell	9.9	9.1
Indiana	9.9	13.0
Catholic U.	10.3	13.8
California (Berkeley)	10.3	11.9
UCLA	10.5	12.6
Minnesota	10.5	12.4
Illinois	10.7	13.9
Vanderbilt	11.0	9.0
State U. of Iowa	11.1	12.0
Ohio State	11.3	13.3
Washington	11.3	13.4
Pennsylvania	11.5	18.4
Radcliffe	—	11.5
Michigan	11.7	15.2
Northwestern	11.8	15.0
Chicago	11.9	15.8
Stanford	12.1	11.9
North Carolina	12.3	10.8
Columbia	12.5	15.1
Boston U.	12.6	15.8
USC	13.5	18.1
Texas	13.7	19.1
Fordham	13.9	17.6
NYU	14.0	18.2

The figures for the male candidates obviously are more stable since, as we have noted elsewhere, women receive less than 9 per cent of the doctorates granted in the humanistic disciplines. This table reveals some fairly wide discrepancies in the average lag time for different institutions. The Ivy League universities of the East all appear among the first half dozen, and there is a general tendency for the state universities to have a somewhat longer lag time than private institutions. But this is, at best, only a suggestive trend since Chicago, Stanford, Columbia, and NYU are among the lowest ten. Of considerably more importance is the difference in lag time displayed by male and female doctorate recipients. The lag time for women is appreciably greater than that for men in virtually all institutions.

While differences in lag time among universities are not clearly related to meaningful variables, the lag-time difference among fields is of greater significance. Here we note, in Table 45, the average lag time for our five humanistic fields.

TABLE 45. Average lag time, in years, by humanistic field.

	Male	Female
Philosophy	9.81	13.48
History	10.69	13.17
Foreign languages & literature	11.12	14.75
English	11.27	14.64
Fine arts & music	12.42	13.60

Philosophy, on the average, provides the swiftest route to the doctorate; arts and music presents the longest. This conforms with the data reported by Harmon and Soldz employing a somewhat different sample. We also note here the persistently higher lag time, of roughly three years, for female scholars in all fields. It is worth observing that individual departments may vary appreciably in the same institutions. There is a clear suggestion that the lag time is primarily a product of departmental policy and practice, and only secondarily determined by institutional policy or field of study.

One must be impressed with the extraordinary lapse of time, in general, between the baccalaureate and the doctoral degree in the humanities. Bernard Berelson, in his 1960 review of graduate education in the United States, points to the reduction of this interval in all fields as one of the foremost reformations to be desired. It seems particularly appropriate to emphasize here that the humanistic disciplines, more than the scientific disciplines, impose a personal and psychological strain upon their adherents through this policy of protracted training and the deferment of the doctorate. Berelson's strongest criticism of graduate education applies with particular force to the humanistic disciplines.

The picture of graduate education in the humanities can be further illuminated by presenting the ratio of doctorates granted in the sciences to those in the humanities among our thirty most productive universities. For this purpose I have employed the data assembled by

the National Academy of Sciences, reporting doctorates granted from
1936 to 1956. Table 46 shows the numbers of doctorates granted in

TABLE 46. Ph.D.'s granted in the sciences and
humanities, 1936-56, and their ratio.

Institution	No. Ph.D.'s (Sciences)	No. Ph.D.'s (Humanities)	Ratio Sci./Hum.
Public			
Minnesota	1,760	248	7.10
Cornell	2,212	318	6.96
Ohio State	1,758	261	6.74
Illinois	2,411	404	5.97
Wisconsin	2,807	591	4.75
California (Berkeley)	2,185	551	3.97
UCLA	536	138	3.88
Michigan	1,700	448	3.79
Washington	504	144	3.50
Texas	661	294	2.25
Indiana	412	183	2.25
State U. of Iowa	791	439	1.80
North Carolina	374	327	1.14
TOTAL	18,111	4,346	4.17
Private			
Johns Hopkins	851	256	3.32
Stanford	802	283	2.83
Northwestern	704	261	2.70
Duke	421	157	2.68
NYU	743	287	2.59
Chicago	1,578	664	2.38
Princeton	769	378	2.03
Pennsylvania	732	468	1.57
Yale	1,116	776	1.43
Harvard	1,429	1,171	1.22
USC	219	185	1.18
Columbia	1,496	1,302	1.15
Vanderbilt	125	138	0.91
Boston U.	128	176	0.73
Radcliffe	103	147	0.70
TOTAL	11,216	6,649	1.69
Catholic			
Catholic U.	224	421	0.53
Fordham	191	193	0.99
TOTAL	415	614	0.68

the sciences and the humanities, and their ratio for public, private, and Catholic universities among our top thirty institutions.

This ratio almost directly parallels the ratios presented in Chapter 3, where a similar report was made on baccalaureates continuing to the doctorate in science and those continuing in the humanities. (Cf. Table 17.)

It will be observed that the composite index for all publicly supported institutions is 4.17; for private institutions this figure is 1.69, and for two Catholic universities, .68. The differences among these three composite measures are impressive and correspond roughly to the results obtained in the indices computed for their baccalaureates who continued to the doctorate. Still, there is some overlapping, at least between the public and private groups, but all except four of the public institutions exceed the highest ratio found among the private institutions. For the Catholic institutions, which number only two, the ratio is in both instances less than unity, indicating the predominance of the humanities over the sciences, a condition generally characteristic of Catholic institutions elsewhere.

Subsequently we shall review the position of the humanities in public and private institutions. We need only observe here that the basic differences in commitment, especially among the better-known institutions of both classes, is clear. It is our private universities that, in the main, afford the most hospitable climate for the humanities, while the sciences tend to predominate in the state universities.

Still one further indication of the comparative position of the humanities and other fields of scholarship may be gathered from Table 47, which presents the mean age of doctorate recipients in major areas and in our five humanistic fields for 1958-59.

TABLE 47. Mean age of those who received
Ph.D.'s in 1958-59, by field.

	Mean Age
History	35.21
Fine arts & music	35.93
Foreign languages and literature	35.84
English literature	35.04
Philosophy	33.60
Physical sciences	30.6[a]
Life sciences	32.5[a]
Behavioral sciences	33.3[a]

[a] National Academy, Science Directory, 1958-59, p.14.

It is clear that the youngest doctorates are, on the average, found in the physical sciences, then in the life sciences, thereafter in the behavioral sciences, and finally in the humanities. Except for philosophy, the mean age in all of our humanistic fields exceeds thirty-five years, approximately five years more than the average in the physical sciences.

In Chapter 6, I have presented data dealing with the undergraduate origins of scholars who had recently received a notable award from the American Council of Learned Societies. A consideration of such persons was undertaken on the assumption that they represented a particularly distinguished and promising group of scholars in the humanities who might be compared roughly with the general population of

TABLE 48. Doctoral origins of recent ACLS awardees.

Institutions Among the Top 30		*Other Institutions*	
Harvard	60	Virginia	3
Yale	37	Bryn Mawr	2
Columbia	36	Western Reserve	2
Princeton	18	Rochester	2
Chicago	16	New Mexico	2
California (Berkeley)	10	Brown	1
Wisconsin	10	Nebraska	1
Michigan	9	Syracuse	1
Pennsylvania	7	Howard	1
Radcliffe	5	Oklahoma	1
NYU	5	TCU	1
Cornell	5	Penn. State	1
Illinois	4	Michigan State	1
Johns Hopkins	4	Cincinnati	1
UCLA	3	Colorado U.	1
North Carolina	3	Pittsburgh	1
Ohio State	3	Washington U.	1
Washington U.	3	Tulane	1
Stanford	2	Clark	1
Boston U.	2	Emory	1
Indiana	2		26
Texas	1		
Northwestern	1	Foreign institutions	39
Duke	1		
	247	No formal doctorate	18
		Doctorate before 1936	67
			150

Ph.D.'s in the humanities. Here it is possible for me to present data on their doctoral origins.

Table 48 sets forth a listing of the institutions granting doctorates to the ACLS scholars. Here again, the Ivy League institutions such as Harvard, Yale, Columbia, and Princeton conspicuously head the group. Harvard claims no less than 60 of the 397 scholars; no state university has more than 10 scholars. Once again the distribution of these elite humanistic scholars shows the same pattern as that for the origins of Ph.D.'s generally, though in a more exaggerated form.

Finally, it may be interesting to compare this list of institutions from which ACLS scholars came with the thirty institutions granting the largest number of doctorates in the humanities. In Table 38, two Catholic institutions, Fordham and Catholic University, were numbered among the top thirty institutions. Neither of these institutions is represented in Table 48, and it may be observed that none of their doctorates is among the 397 ACLS scholars under consideration. This fact is a further confirmation of the degree to which Catholic humanism moves independently from the main course of humanistic scholarship in other quarters.

8

MIGRATION AND CAREER PATTERNS

One persistent question raised among humanists is the quality of students attracted to their disciplines as compared with others. While there appears to have been no definitive study of this problem, at least partial light has been cast upon it. D. L. Wolfle presents data, drawn from a selected group of colleges and universities, that bears upon this issue.[1] Using the Army General Classification Test as a measure of intellectual abilities, he reports the distribution of scores for individual fields and for general areas of the curriculum and for both baccalaureates and graduate students. Students of the physical sciences, both at the baccalaureate level and at the graduate level, have the highest scores, but closely thereafter come the biological and social sciences as well as the humanities. It is the applied fields, such as agriculture, home economics, commerce, dentistry, that appear to fall below the level of the liberal arts. Differences among the several fields of the humanities are slight and do not deserve reporting here. So far as Wolfle's study indicates it appears that the humanities are claiming their share of top intellectual material both at the undergraduate and at the graduate level, and that they are exceeded to a meaningful degree only by the physical sciences and possibly by psychology.

Wolfle offers some further data of interest that relates the position in the high-school graduating class to the field of baccalaureate major.[2] Of the twenty-two classifications recognized in the data, philosophy, languages, English, and fine arts occupy respectively the first, third, sixth, and seventh positions. Only history, among the humanities, falls among the lower half. These figures are not of great importance though they tend to confirm the view that the humanities are attracting talented intellectual material to a creditable degree.

Finally, Wolfle presents some data on the percentage of students, graduating in the humanities and other fields, who continue to the doc-

[1] Dael Lee Wolfle, *America's Resources of Specialized Talent* (Harper, 1954), p. 199.
[2] *Ibid.*, p. 206.

torate degree.[3] Among the natural sciences, the percentage obtaining a doctorate is the highest. Among the social sciences and humanities, the percentages are approximately equal and lower than for natural sciences. In the applied fields, the percentage of undergraduate majors continuing is significantly less.

A more recent study of interest, done by D. L. Thistlethwaite on winners and near-winners of National Merit Scholarships, shows that of his sample of 1,500, 52 per cent selected majors in the natural and biological sciences, 18 per cent in the social sciences, and 20 per cent in the humanities.[4] However, he notes that the proportion of females in the natural sciences is lower than in the humanities. This finding suggests that in most recent times the sciences have increasingly attracted talented undergraduates. Moreover, the proportion of highly talented females in the humanities has been higher than in the sciences.

L. R. Harmon has assembled information from questionnaires returned by Ph.D.'s of the year 1958.[5] His results are not broken down by particular fields of the humanities, but he does present figures for arts and humanities that generally confirm the reports of Wolfle. Thus, with respect to intelligence scores, scholars in the arts and humanities are slightly below those in the physical sciences, about equal to those in the social sciences, and significantly ahead of those in all other fields in this classification. They hold a similar rank with respect to their high-school class. Again we find Wolfle's observation confirmed to the effect that the number of doctorates in the physical sciences is significantly higher than those for arts and humanities, while those in the arts and humanities exceed biological sciences and other fields. Finally, Harmon presents data on the regional distribution of doctorates that indicates a particularly high rate for the New England and Mid-Atlantic states in the humanities.

This chapter presents a variety of information characterizing the career patterns and personal qualities of students in the humanities; the information is drawn from diverse sources but primarily from the National Academy of Sciences, which, beginning in 1957, sent fairly detailed questionnaires to all recipients of the doctoral degree in humani-

---

[3] *Ibid.,* p. 45.
[4] D. L. Thistlethwaite, "Merit Scholarships and the Higher Education of Gifted Students," *Journal of Higher Education,* XXX, 6 (1959), 295-304.
[5] L. R. Harmon, "High School Backgrounds of Science Doctorates," *Science,* CXXXIII, 3454 (1961), 679-88.

ties from American universities. In some instances comparisons can be made among scientists, social scientists, and those in the humanities.

Of first interest is the "migration data," describing the movement of scholars from one geographic region to another in the course of their studies. From this source I have compiled three tables that include virtually all Ph.D.'s in the humanities granted between 1957 through 1959. Table 49a shows the regional location of the scholar's high school tabulated against the regional location of his undergraduate institution. The nine regions are those recognized by the United States Bureau of the Census.

It will probably be no surprise that in approximately 75 per cent of all instances the baccalaureate region and the high-school region are the same. Still, there are some variations in this regard that deserve comment. Thus, the Mountain states appear to be most prone to export their high-school graduates for baccalaureate training elsewhere, whereas the Pacific Coast and the West South Central seem most disposed to retain their high-school graduates for baccalaureate training in their area. Usually, when students take their baccalaureate work in a region other than that of their high school, the new region tends to be an adjacent territory. For example, an appreciable exchange occurs between New England and the Middle Atlantic area. The Pacific and Mountain regions also show a substantial linkage. However, the relative self-containment of each of these regions remains.

Table 49b shows the percentages contributed by the different regions at the high-school and baccalaureate levels. Three of the regions—New England, Middle Atlantic, and East North Central—account for the high-school origins of 59.5 per cent of all our humanistic scholars. The most productive region, Middle Atlantic, is characterized by high population density and urbanization.

Comparable figures for baccalaureate origins show the same degree of concentration in these three regions. Notably, there is a substantial exodus from the Middle Atlantic states to New England, as students move from the high schools of New York, Pennsylvania, and New Jersey to the humanities-minded colleges of New England.

Table 50a is a cross-tabulation of baccalaureate and doctoral regions. Far greater mobility is shown here than in the preceding table, where migration from high school to college was presented. In slightly less than 50 per cent of the cases in Table 50a the baccalaureate and the doctoral regions are the same. The regions most notable for export of

TABLE 49a. Migration by region—high school to B.A. institutions.

High School Region[a]

B.A. Region		1 New England	2 Middle Atlantic	3 East North Central	4 West North Central	5 South Atlantic	6 East South Central	7 West South Central	8 Mountain	9 Pacific
1	No.	141	59	21	2	10	3	2	3	8
	%	75.0	11.3	6.6	1.3	5.8	4.4	2.0	5.9	5.3
2	No.	21	360	15	5	7	3	2	1	7
	%	11.2	69.2	4.7	3.2	4.1	4.4	2.0	2.0	4.6
3	No.	13	45	255	15	13	3	7	5	6
	%	6.9	8.7	79.7	9.6	7.6	4.4	6.9	9.8	3.9
4	No.	1	2	10	119	3	2	4	2	3
	%	.5	.4	3.1	75.8	1.8	2.9	4.0	3.9	2.0
5	No.	6	40	8	1	127	7	1	1	1
	%	3.2	7.8	2.5	.6	74.3	1.0	1.0	2.0	.7
6	No.	3	3	1	2	8	45	2	—	—
	%	1.6	.6	.3	1.3	4.7	65.2	2.0	—	—
7	No.	—	2	2	3	—	5	82	1	2
	%	—	.4	.6	1.9	—	7.2	81.2	2.0	1.3
8	No.	2	—	3	3	—	—	—	29	4
	%	1.1	—	.9	1.9	—	—	—	56.9	2.6
9	No.	1	9	5	7	3	1	1	9	121
	%	.5	1.7	1.6	4.5	1.8	1.4	1.0	17.6	80.0
TOTAL	No.	188	520	320	157	171	69	101	51	152

[a] U.S. Census classification.

TABLE 49b. Migration by region—high school to B.A. institution (totals).

		New England	Middle Atlantic	East North Central	West North Central	South Atlantic	East South Central	West South Central	Mountain	Pacific
High school region	No.	188	520	320	157	171	69	101	51	152
	%	10.9	30.1	18.5	9.1	9.9	4.0	5.8	2.9	8.8
B.A. region	No.	249	421	362	146	192	64	97	41	157
	%	14.4	24.3	20.9	8.4	11.1	3.7	5.6	2.4	9.1

TABLE 50a. Migration by region—B.A. institution to Ph.D. institution.

Ph.D. Region		1 New England	2 Middle Atlantic	3 East North Central	4 West North Central	5 South Atlantic	6 East South Central	7 West South Central	8 Mountain	9 Pacific
1	No.	132	64	46	19	22	7	5	3	16
	%	49.6	13.9	11.3	12.2	11.0	10.6	5.1	6.3	8.4
2	No.	57	241	53	16	40	8	9	6	25
	%	21.4	52.6	13.0	10.3	20.0	12.1	9.1	12.5	13.2
3	No.	38	63	216	30	24	9	12	6	19
	%	14.3	13.8	52.9	19.2	12.0	13.6	12.1	12.5	10.0
4	No.	6	17	37	61	6	2	4	5	11
	%	2.3	3.7	9.1	39.1	3.0	3.0	4.0	10.4	5.8
5	No.	15	41	23	7	90	18	8	1	7
	%	5.6	9.0	5.6	4.5	45.0	27.3	8.1	2.1	3.1
6	No.	—	1	1	1	6	15	4	1	—
	%		.2	.2	.6	3.0	22.7	4.0	2.1	
7	No.	—	4	4	9	5	5	51	1	2
	%		.9	1.0	5.8	2.5	7.6	51.5	2.1	1.1
8	No.	2	2	3	6	2	1	3	11	3
	%	.8	.4	.7	3.8	1.0	1.5	3.0	22.9	1.6
9	No.	16	25	25	7	5	1	3	14	107
	%	6.0	5.6	6.1	4.5	2.5	1.5	3.0	29.2	56.3
TOTAL	No.	266	458	408	156	200	66	99	48	190

TABLE 50b. Migration by region—B.A. institution to Ph. D. institution (totals).

		New England	Middle Atlantic	East North Central	West North Central	South Atlantic	East South Central	West South Central	Mountain	Pacific
B.A. Region	No.	266	458	408	156	200	66	99	48	190
	%	14.1	24.2	21.6	8.2	10.6	3.5	5.2	2.5	10.0
Ph.D Region	No.	314	455	417	149	210	29	81	33	203
	%	16.6	24.1	22.1	7.9	11.1	1.5	4.3	1.7	10.7

TABLE 51a. Migration by region—Ph.D. institution to job.

	Job Region		1 New England	2 Middle Atlantic	3 East North Central	4 West North Central	5 South Atlantic	6 East South Central	7 West South Central	8 Mountain	9 Pacific
	1	No.	106	39	17	5	6	—	1	—	5
		%	42.7	11.3	6.0	5.0	3.7	—	2.4	—	3.9
	2	No.	46	188	21	4	18	1	1	2	5
		%	18.5	54.6	7.4	4.0	11.2	11.1	2.4	13.3	3.9
	3	No.	37	29	143	26	15	2	3	3	20
		%	14.9	8.4	50.7	26.0	9.3	22.2	7.3	20.0	15.6
	4	No.	10	11	22	31	4	—	7	3	7
		%	4.0	3.2	7.8	31.0	2.5	—	17.1	20.0	5.5
	5	No.	18	34	25	7	81	—	2	1	—
		%	7.8	10.0	8.9	7.0	50.3	—	4.9	6.7	—
	6	No.	2	10	12	1	13	3	3	—	2
		%	.8	2.9	4.3	1.0	8.1	33.3	7.3	—	1.6
	7	No.	6	13	12	7	14	2	23	—	6
		%	2.4	3.8	4.3	7.0	8.7	22.2	56.1	—	4.7
	8	No.	3	6	7	7	4	1	1	2	15
		%	1.2	1.7	2.5	7.0	2.5	11.1	2.4	13.3	11.7
	9	No.	20	14	23	12	6	—	—	4	68
		%	8.1	4.1	8.2	12.0	3.7	—	—	26.7	53.1
	TOTAL	No.	248	344	282	100	161	9	41	15	128

Ph.D. Region

TABLE 51b. Migration by region—Ph.D. institution to job (totals).

		New England	Middle Atlantic	East North Central	West North Central	South Atlantic	East South Central	West South Central	Mountain	Pacific
Ph.D. region	No.	248	344	282	100	161	9	41	15	128
	%	18.7	25.9	21.2	7.5	12.1	0.7	3.1	1.3	9.6
Job region	No.	179	286	278	95	168	46	83	46	147
	%	13.5	21.5	20.9	7.2	12.7	3.5	6.3	3.5	11.1

baccalaureate scholars to doctoral study elsewhere turn out to be the Mountain region and the Central Southern states. The Northeast and Pacific sections retain a high percentage of their baccalaureates for doctoral training. The same, interestingly enough, may be said for the West South, although the numbers here are less reliable.

I earlier noted that when there is migration from region to region, adjacent regions usually benefit, at least with respect to high-school and baccalaureate training. We see this same tendency here. Thus 85 per cent of the people who take the baccalaureate in New England take their doctorate in the northeastern section of the country, comprising the first three census areas. Similarly, 80 per cent of those from the Middle Atlantic states remain there for their doctoral training. Approximately the same may be said for the East North Central states.

The Pacific Coast presents a rather interesting pattern. It draws very substantially from the northeastern seaboard, despite its geographical remoteness, claiming approximately 17 per cent of its doctoral candidates from the first three census regions. On the other hand, the Pacific region exports over 30 per cent of its baccalaureates to the universities of the northeast for doctorates.

Table 50b offers occasion for further comment. The percentages of baccalaureates given for each of our nine regions very closely approach the totals presented in the preceding table, as indeed they should. They would, in fact, be identical, except for some small differences in sampling due to the failure of all doctoral recipients to report.

The percentages indicating doctoral origins display again a very heavy concentration in the northeastern sections of the country, especially New England. Thus only slightly less than 11 per cent of the questionnaire respondents took their high-school training here; about 14 per cent took their baccalaureate here; and almost 17 per cent received their doctoral here. There is some clear evidence, therefore, of migration into New England as more advanced stages of humanistic education are pursued.

Table 51a shows the movement from region of doctoral degree to region of employment. Here we are dealing with the 1,328 respondents to the questionnaire distributed by the National Academy of Sciences who were able to report employment at the time the questionnaire was submitted. Here, as in the other two tables, one sees that people generally find employment in the region in which they received a doctorate. Interestingly, though, people who have taken their doctorates in the northeastern regions of the country tend to move elsewhere for their employment. Table 51b demonstrates very clearly that New England and the Middle Atlantic regions are a training ground for humanistic scholars, who tend thereafter to move elsewhere for the assumption of their academic posts.

The National Academy of Sciences has provided rather detailed data covering the regions of birth, high school, baccalaureate degree, and doctorate, for humanistic scholars in particular fields. However, there appear to be few if any, important differences between the several fields. They all show a fairly steady movement toward the Northeast and the Pacific Coast, as successive stages of educational progress are examined. We shall, therefore, pass over this data without further comment.

Information concerning the socioeconomic background of humanistic scholars, or of those majoring in the humanities, has not been directly available to me. However, several studies, such as that being continued by the National Opinion Research Council, suggest no significant difference in the amount of education or income of the families from which humanistic scholars and scientists derive. The trends suggest, if anything, a higher socioeconomic background for humanists than for other fields. Wolfle presents data showing that, in comparison with applied fields of study, students in the arts and sciences come from families of higher economic standing. The fragmentary evidence, therefore, suggests that the humanities recruit their numbers from average to higher economic and educational strata. The type of community from which humanists come is similar to those of other doctoral recipients, according to the NORC study. A special exception has to be made, however, in the case of the fine arts, whose scholars are drawn more frequently from larger urban centers.

Considering that Catholic institutions, as we have seen, are particularly disposed to support the humanities, one might expect that the percentage of Catholics attracted to this area of scholarship would be greater than that attracted to the sciences. Limited data from the National Opinion Research Center[6] supports this view and shows, indeed, that on the basis of their rather constricted sample Protestants and Jews are proportionally smaller than Catholics, among those continuing in graduate school in the humanities.

[6] National Opinion Research Center, *Great Aspirations,* Report #82 (U. of Chicago, 1961).

TABLE 52. Employer by field for humanistic doctorates, 1957-59 (in per cent).

| | College & Univ. | Other Educ. | Government | | | Non-Profit | Indust. & Bus. | Self | Other | No. |
			U.S.	Foreign	State & Local					
History	85.02	5.70	4.01	—	.21	3.38	1.05	.21	.42	474
Fine arts & music	86.59	5.49	—	1.22	—	2.44	1.22	1.83	1.22	164
Foreign literature	92.55	4.04	.93	—	—	1.24	.31	.31	.62	322
English literature	94.38	1.55	.58	.19	—	.19	1.55	.78	.78	516
Philosophy	90.51	3.16	—	—	—	3.80	.63	.63	1.27	158

94

Table 52 shows the proportion of humanists entering employment in different occupations, 1957-59. Among all humanistic fields teaching is overwhelmingly the selected means of livelihood. This fact is in rather sharp contrast to the natural sciences, and still more so to the applied fields, where far more than half the doctorates pursue nonacademic vocations. The dedication of humanists to the teaching profession is supported by at least two other sources, namely, by the attitudes of humanistic administrators and scholars reported by Berelson and by the analysis of the vocational commitments to different areas of learning reported by NORC.

Humanists are naturally interested in knowing how they might differ from other professions with respect to attributes of temperament and personality. A number of studies have been conducted on students regarding the nature of scholars in the humanities, many of which are reviewed in *The American College*.[7] I have made two studies involving the examination of personality differences between undergraduates concentrated in different curricular areas.[8] It would probably be inappropriate to undertake here an extensive survey of this literature, but it should be emphasized that abundant evidence indicates widespread and important differences in values, attitudes, and temperaments between humanists and scholars in other fields, be they mature scholars or students in the humanities. These studies indicate that, on the average, humanists appear to be more introverted, more impulsive, less interested in objects, more interested in ideas, more personalized in their approach to other people, more vivid in their imagination and imagery, more unconventional, and more concerned with abstraction. On many personality tests they show a more ready access to their feelings and emotions than do scholars in other areas. In short, there appears to be no question among psychologists that the humanities both attract and develop qualities of personality that distinguish humanists as a group.

---

[7] C. Bereiter and M. B. Freedman, "Fields of Study and the People in Them." Chapter 17 in R. Nevitt Sanford, ed., *The American College* (Wiley, 1962).
[8] Robert H. Knapp, "The Non-Intellective Determinents of Scientific Interest," O.N.R. Report NONR (oo), 1951, and "A Factor Analysis of Thorndike's Ratings of Eminent Men," *Journal of Social Psychology*, LVI (1962), 67-71.

9

DESIGN OF THE CASE STUDIES

The preceding seven chapters have been devoted primarily to evaluating statistical data that shed light on the educational origins of American humanists. These data have repeatedly pointed to a major distinction between two types of institutions: privately supported institutions of high cost, characteristically, but not exclusively, represented by the Ivy League universities of the East; and the great publicly supported state universities, represented typically by those in the Midwest and the West. The first of these types is a fertile and prolific source of humanistic scholars, though the numbers of their students, graduate and undergraduate, are relatively small as compared with the system of state and land grant universities. On the other hand, it may be said of the state universities that here the emphasis upon humanistic learning is not central, but, in the main, incidental. The yield of humanistic scholars from these institutions constitutes a secondary emphasis whereas the sciences, technologies, and professions are primary. Surely a visitor to this country, asked to survey the quality of higher education in America, would be impressed with the essential difference in style and commitment of these two classes of institutions. The next three chapters will consider in some detail the fate of the humanities within the intellectual and institutional climate of eight universities drawn from these two classes.

But first it might be useful to review some of the statistical evidence that so strongly points to a sharp division of universities into two major classes, with particular reference to their output of humanistic scholars. This evidence may be summarized as follows:

(1) We saw, from a mathematically evolved typology presented in Chapter 2, that institutions notable for a high yield of humanists as compared with other types of scholars were heavily represented by Ivy League colleges and universities. State universities, on the other hand, were in the main identified with another style of scholarly production, tending to emphasize the production of scholars in the sciences and technologies.

(2) Chapter 3 presented a series of lists showing the colleges and universities that have produced, from among their baccalaureates, the greatest *number* of scholars in the humanities in recent decades. Conspicuous here are a number of Ivy League colleges and universities that despite their small size appear consistently at or near the top of our lists, both composite and by field of scholarship.

(3) In Chapter 4 it was clearly established that a high *rate* in the production of humanistic scholars in liberal arts colleges was associated in location in the north eastern section of the country with private nondenominational control, and with high cost of tuition and attendance. More specifically, Eastern Ivy League colleges were shown to have the consistently high indices of humanistic production.

(4) Comparable findings for a large sample of universities were presented in Chapter 5, showing that here, as among liberal arts colleges, the Ivy League institutions of the East were particularly distinguished.

(5) I have also been able to demonstrate, in Chapter 6, that private universities and state universities differ markedly in their relative contributions to the humanities and the sciences. Ivy League universities, in contrast to state universities, are noted for the relatively high proportion of their baccalaureates who continue to the doctorate in the humanities as compared with the sciences.

(6) Chapter 7 revealed two major pathways and one minor pathway to the doctorate, namely, the Ivy League, the state university, and the Catholic pathways. From the baccalaureate to the doctorate, there appears to be relatively little cross-over between these three systems.

(7) Finally, in Chapter 8 we saw that fellows of the American Council of Learned Societies in recent years reveal an extraordinary concentration among baccalaureates from Ivy League institutions. Still more incisive is the concentration of doctorates from this class of university.

In selecting universities to be visited for the purpose of inquiring into the relation of humanistic scholarship and recruitment to the type of the institution, I was guided by the considerations just set forth. Before justifying particular selections, however, I should like to say that I had no real hope of evaluating the structure, direction, and performance of particular departments, since this obviously is far beyond the scope that time and circumstances permit. It would be vain and presumptuous to venture, for example, a historical review and critique of the history department at Harvard, or the fine arts department at Yale, and above all to ascribe responsibilities to particular individuals either for accomplishment or for its lack. Rather it has been my purpose to review the total climate and history of the institution, the quality of its students, certain special features of administrative policy, and, in conspicuous cases, distinctive organizational factors that relate to its record in the recruitment and training of humanistic scholars. Beyond this, and particularly considering the fact that I am not myself in the humanistic disciplines, I hoped to gain from a series of interviews with humanistic scholars and administrators some general conceptions of the outlook, attitudes, and hopes that characterize this segment of scholarship and mark it off, in particular, from the sciences.

In selecting the cases to be presently reviewed I attempted to pick relatively pure specimens of the two great university types in America. It is my presumption that the forces operating at Harvard and Yale, and possibly at Stanford, are shared by many other colleges and universities of similar general style and commitment. Similarly, my reviews of Wisconsin, Indiana, Ohio State, and the University of California at Berkeley are pursued in the expectation that these represent fairly typical variants of the great state universities. Thus, while these case studies may possess particularistic interest, they should be seen as examples of two much larger classes of institutions of higher learning, holding aside, for a moment, the smaller class of Catholic institutions exemplified by Catholic University of America. The case studies hence will show, to some extent, why the statistics examined in previous chapters look as they do. In short, I shall try to answer the question "What are the forces that have shaped the statistics?"

As I have indicated, eight major American universities were visited in pursuance of these aims. As representatives of Ivy League universities I selected Yale and Harvard, excluding Princeton for the obvious reason that it sponsored this project. Also included among eastern private universities was Catholic University of America, the foremost graduate institution of its type in America, holding, as shall be seen, a special preeminence in American Catholic education. As representative of midwestern state universities, I have selected three. The first of these, the University of Wisconsin, was selected by virtue of its early emergence as a major intellectual center in the region and its combining a land grant tradition with a yet older tradition of a state university. Second was Indiana University, chosen as a state university without land grant affiliation whose record, historically speaking, was relatively undistinguished, though in the present decade it is a vigorous newcomer to the ranks of top-flight state universities. The third selection was Ohio State University, chosen as an institution conceived and developed under the land grant tradition. Ohio State remains, more than the other two state universities, committed to the ideals of public service and the advancement of useful and technical arts, and stands as one of the most thriving examples of a land grant institution in the Midwest. From the Pacific region I selected the University of California at Berkeley, as an example of a state-supported institution, to be compared with Stanford, which bears some obvious resemblances to the Ivy League universities of the East. But it may be noted that Berkeley and Stanford admit of many exceptions to any stereotyped conception of the state and Ivy League university.

I spent approximately ten days at each institution, during which period interviews were conducted with representatives of all major humanistic departments. On occasion I talked with members of the social sciences and also the natural sciences, and it was regular policy to interview public relations officers, directors of admissions, and graduate deans. In most cases no prescribed schedule was followed, and an effort was made to obtain a free and candid expression from the informant about the position of the humanities in his institution. I have adopted the general policy of not citing the names of persons interviewed, and above all, of not ascribing particular credit or fault for developments within an institution. This has been done because of the wish not to violate certain confidences or become involved in unwarranted and unsustained conclusions and judgments.

For purposes of presentation I shall first report on two Ivy League universities, Yale and Harvard, and thereafter Catholic University, in a single chapter. Then, I shall report on a Pacific Coast pair, Stanford and the University of California at Berkeley, both of which are somewhere between Ivy League and state universities in terms of humanistic production and environment. Finally, I shall report on three midwestern state universities, Indiana, Wisconsin, and Ohio.

At the risk of some repetition, I should like to present here a particularly revealing table, showing one of the indices of hospitality to the humanities, namely, the ratio of those continuing to a doctorate in the sciences to those continuing in the humanities, as well as the ratio of actual doctorates granted in these fields, 1936-56. In Table 53 it will be observed that in the first three institutions, both the baccalaureate and doctoral ratios are notably low, eminently so in the case of Catholic University.

TABLE 53. Science/humanities ratios for eight
institutions visited.

	Baccalaureates Earning Doctorate	Doctorates Granted
Yale	1.5	1.4
Harvard	1.6	1.2
Catholic U.	.4	.5
Stanford	2.3	2.8
California (Berkeley)	4.6	4.0
Indiana	3.2	2.2
Wisconsin	4.6	4.7
Ohio State	6.3	6.7

The first column indicates the number of baccalaureates continuing to a doctorate in the sciences divided by the number continuing in the humanities at the baccalaureate institution or elsewhere. The second column supplies a figure representing the number of actual doctorates granted in the sciences divided by those granted in the humanities. For convenience I shall refer to these respectively as the baccalaureate and doctorate ratios. The two Pacific Coast institutions show Stanford only slightly higher than the Ivy League institutions with respect to these measures, while the University of California at Berkeley shows roughly twice these ratios, indicating that the sciences there occupy a more predominant position, both with respect to the scholarly careers selected by its baccalaureates and to doctoral degrees actually granted there. Again, among the midwestern institutions the ratios in all instances are substantially greater than for any private institution. Thus, this presentation of cases moves, roughly, from those that show a high humanistic emphasis to those of low humanistic commitment; still, one should interpret these ratios in the light of the difference between private and public institutional purposes and structure. One should also note here that the two kinds of ratios bear a striking correspondence to each other, suggesting a very clear stylistic congruence between the quality of undergraduate interest and the pattern of distribution of doctorate degrees granted.

One further bit of statistical information can usefully be presented at this juncture. In reviewing the attainments of the eight universities in the subsequent chapters, I present a record of what part of their graduates continue to the doctorate in the humanities, as well as the number of doctorates they have themselves awarded in these areas. These figures can usefully be interpreted in the light of those presented in Table 54, which shows the numbers and percentages of students in each of the five fields who took a doctorate in all American institutions from 1936 to 1956 in the humanities.

TABLE 54. Number and per cent of students in all American institutions taking a doctorate in the five humanistic fields, 1936-56.

B.A.	Number	Per cent
Foreign languages & literature	2,968	23
History	4,071	31
English	4,047	31
Fine arts & music	825	6
Philosophy	1,146	9

It will be observed that history and English each account for 31 per cent of the total, and in most institutions are the two most productive departments. Philosophy and art, on the other hand, are numerically small disciplines, and we should not expect, except in unusual circumstances, to find a large number of students receiving a doctorate from any of our eight institutions. The tables presented hereafter should be evaluated in the light of the percentages given in Table 54.

CARL A. RUDISILL LIBRARY
LENOIR RHYNE COLLEGE

❧ 10 ❧

THREE EASTERN PRIVATE UNIVERSITIES

This chapter is a report on visits made to Catholic University of America, Yale University, and Harvard University. The inclusion of Catholic University with Harvard and Yale is partly a matter of editorial convenience, for it is clearly dissimilar in type and history. Yet its inclusion has some genuine justification. As shown at the end of the last chapter, these three institutions appear to emphasize the humanities, as compared to the sciences, in a distinctive degree. Beyond this, they are all located within the "fertile crescent" that begins with Harvard's Widener Library and extends to the Library of Congress in Washington, and is circumscribed by the Appalachians on the west. It is from this region, as the statistics show, that scholars in the humanities emerge in particularly high proportion, and it is here that the most famous libraries and fine arts collections are distributed.

Catholic University

The Catholic University of America in Washington, D.C., is without question the foremost contender among church-affiliated universities for a high position in the humanities. The number of doctorates granted in all fields greatly exceeds that of any other Catholic institution, and the proportion of them in humanistic studies is notable. The university was founded shortly before the turn of the century, under the special auspices of papal mandate. In this respect it differs from all other Catholic universities in the country, which are supported either by teaching orders or by a local diocese. Not only does Catholic University benefit from the special dignity of its charter and its transcendence of both clerical orders and diocesan divisions, but it also has the unique privilege of claiming for its support one annual church collection a year from all Catholic churches throughout the nation. Its Board of Regents, composed of the Council of American Catholic Bishops, lends it further prestige. An indication of Catholic University's pre-eminent position among Catholic institutions is the fact that it is currently charged with the preparation of a revision of *The Catholic Encyclopedia.* Finally, its position among American Catholic universities and colleges is greatly strengthened by the system of affiliated colleges that serve as training grounds for its graduate departments. Among the affiliates, too, are secondary schools and junior colleges whose recognition by Catholic University is tantamount to accreditization within the Catholic educational system.

Catholic University was modeled after European predecessors, notably the University of Louvain. It presents a radical and striking contrast to virtually all American Protestant universities and certainly to nonsectarian and public institutions. These points of contrast are so numerous and embracing that a full catalog of them would require considerable space. For example, the chief administrative officer and rector is a papal appointee. The curriculum, divided into a number of colleges, itself provides an interesting study in contrast. Thus, a special college was set up to deal with the social sciences in the late 1930's. Another college is entirely devoted to philosophy; still another to sacred theology. But side by side with these, which are devoted to conventional traditional scholarship, stand the College of Nursing, the College of Social Work, and the College of Engineering and Architecture, with their avowedly utilitarian and service orientation.

The intermixture of lay and clerical influence is again a special feature of this institution. Approximately one third of the faculty are laymen, a fraction considerably higher than that in most Catholic institutions. Moreover, lay Catholics, in numerous instances, are entrusted with deanships and other high administrative offices. On the other hand there is very little of the democratic and parliamentary freedom in the faculty that characterizes many private nondenominational and even public institutions. Finally, this institution serves in a special sense the higher educational needs of Catholic teaching orders. Indeed, many of its degrees are granted to members of these orders who pursue their higher studies as part of their religious calling.

It should probably be noted that Catholic University is atypical. Like Johns Hopkins and Clark, it was founded primarily as a graduate institution; only subsequently, again like Johns Hopkins and Clark, did it add an undergraduate division—a division that possessed little or no distinction until the 1930's, and one that appears to have had a very stormy career. But in the 1930's the curriculum was revised, admission standards were more severely enforced, and in 1937 the undergraduate student body became coeducational. Thus, since this decade, the under-graduate student body at Catholic University has become a major and recognized part of the institution. Probably more rigorous standards of admission have been maintained here than at any other Catholic insti-tution in America, and the output of scholars in all fields is higher, with respect to both number and rate than in other Catholic schools.

The undergraduate division of Catholic University is more like a lib-eral arts college, both in point of enrollment and in spirit, than a large university. In the past three decades its annual number of male gradu-ates has ranged from approximately 150 to 300, whereas its female graduates have been about half of these numbers. Still, as Table 55 shows, a very substantial number of graduates have continued to the doctoral level in the humanities with a singular and concentrated em-phasis in philosophy. As noted before, philosophy is normally one of the numerically smallest of the humanistic disciplines, but at Catholic University more graduates continue to a doctorate in philosophy than in all other humanistic fields combined. The indices for the production of male scholars in the humanities, i.e., rate per thousand male gradu-ates, for Period III is 34.3 and for Period IV 21.4 while the indices for philosophy are the highest of any institution in the country.

TABLE 55. Baccalaureate graduates of Catholic University who continued to a Ph.D. in humanities.

B.A. Year		Foreign Languages	History	English	Fine Arts and Music	Philosophy	Total
Before	M	3	5	1	—	1	10
1926	F	4	3	2	—	—	9
1926-35	M	12	2	3	—	8	25
	F	5	5	2	—	2	14
1936-45	M	7	11	6	—	33	57
	F	5	1	1	—	—	7
1946-59	M	2	2	5	2	14	25
	F	3	—	—	—	2	5

A high number of Catholic University baccalaureates pursue human-istic scholarship. In fact, its science-humanities ratio for B.A.'s continu-ing to the doctorate stands at about 0.6, which is the lowest for any in-stitution of prime significance in the country.

In all these respects, Catholic University seems quite set apart from most American institutions, which are characterized by lower rates of scholarly production, greater emphasis on the sciences and professions, and among the humanities the comparative neglect of philosophy in favor of history, foreign languages, and literature.

The graduate program of Catholic University produces many more Ph.D.'s than any other Catholic institution in America. In the past two and one-half decades, moreover, the ratio of Ph.D.'s granted in the humanities to those in the sciences has been approximately two to one, a ratio higher than any other major institution. Indeed, it represents the extreme of a tendency among Catholic institutions in general to emphasize humanities to the detriment of the sciences. Table 56 shows this tendency in detail.

TABLE 56. Ph.D. degrees granted by
Catholic University.

Ph.D. Year	Physical Sciences	Biological Sciences	Social Sciences	Humanities	Education	Other
1936-42	34	25	68	143	41	98
1943-49	28	10	67	129	28	174
1950-56	96	31	99	149	58	129
TOTAL	158	66	234	421	127	401

Again, Table 57 notes that of the doctorates granted in the humanities, the greatest number is given in the field of philosophy, which accounts for over one third, while almost another third is granted in foreign languages and literature. History places a poor third, English language and literature fourth, while arts and music are represented by a single doctorate between 1936 and 1956. This is an atypical pattern among American institutions, but it parallels the scholarly record of Catholic University's own baccalaureate graduates.

TABLE 57. Ph.D. degrees in humanities granted by
Catholic University.

Ph.D. Year	Foreign Languages	History	English	Fine Arts and Music	Philosophy	Total
1936-42	58	33	17	—	35	143
1943-49	45	28	21	—	35	129
1950-56	30	28	23	1	67	149
TOTAL	133	89	61	1	137	421

The data on recruitment of graduate students by Catholic University, as reported in Chapter 7, reveal that of those who have taken their baccalaureate since 1946 and completed their doctorate by 1959, over one half have come from the South. Fifty-two per cent of its graduate students are recruited from other Catholic institutions, while 34 per cent are its own baccalaureates, leaving only 14 per cent that are recruited from non-Catholic schools.

Finally, it is interesting to note that the lag time in the humanities between baccalaureate and doctorate degrees is not excessively long. One might think it would be, considering the clerical vocation of many students. But, on the basis of limited evidence it appears that Catholic University provides the fastest and one of the most efficient avenues to the doctorate among Catholic universities in America. In this respect it stands ninth among major American universities.

It is probably not profitable, or even just, to attempt a detailed evaluation of the several humanistic departments at Catholic University. But a few general observations are undoubtedly warranted. First, languages, and especially classical languages, achieve not surprisingly a special emphasis, partly in accordance with Catholic tradition, but also as a required subject for clerical personnel. All philosophy courses are taught in both English and Latin. Over the past two decades there has been concentration upon scholarship related to church affairs. The publication of the works of the church fathers and their critical evaluation has been a continuing and notable contribution of the department. The position of the classics department has been further reinforced at the undergraduate level by the language requirement for Latin, maintained until very recently for undergraduate admissions. The department of romance languages likewise has had a significant scholarly stature, and more recently other linguistic innovations, including courses in Russian, have been added to the language offerings. The English and history departments at this institution do not attain the predominance among the humanities that is common in most institutions.

As noted above, an entire college is devoted to philosophy. Furthermore, four years of undergraduate work are required in this area. An investigation of the contents of theses in the philosophy division shows some tendency to concentrate on medieval studies, but this is by no means an exclusive concern. Those who would contend that philosophy at this institution is merely neo-Thomism would find themselves, upon closer investigation, to be much in error. However, to evaluate the quality and meaning of a doctorate degree in philosophy from this institution is somewhat difficult. The number granted in this field from 1936 to 1956 is second only to Columbia and substantially exceeds all other universities in the nation. However, of these doctorates, the majority have been given to members of clerical orders in pursuit of their ecclesiastical disciplines. The question of whether these doctorates attain the standards maintained in other private universities cannot be judged by this writer. But the very special dedication of this university to philosophy is patent.

Music and the arts at Catholic University have obviously achieved no status as scholarly areas for doctoral study. Considering the impressive resources of our national capital in the fine arts, it seems that an opportunity here has been neglected. It should be noted, however, that the active theatre at Catholic University has achieved some renown, even though art, music, and the theatre do not constitute areas of scholarly attainment. It is probably fair to say that in the arts, emphasis is on teacher preparation.

How do other departments stand? The sciences are all competently instructed, but actually can claim no great prestige. There is a very important School of Catholic Theology and Canon Law, probably the most eminent in America, which has granted almost as many doctorates as all the humanities together. The existence of this powerful theological school unquestionably lends some support to instruction in the humanities. On the other hand, the existence of schools of social work, nursing, and education seem to constitute a paradoxical and inconsistent development that is hard to reconcile with the intellectual and scholarly dispositions of the Colleges of Arts and Sciences, Philosophy, and Theology. Such service functions are not to be found, for instance, in European Catholic universities.

In summary, Catholic University is a very special type of institution, representing a largely successful attempt to transplant a European Catholic university to the North American continent. Over the seven decades of its history it has undergone shifts and adjustments that have brought to it an unusual pattern for a Catholic school, combining a small quality undergraduate college with a series of graduate colleges covering an extensive range from social work to theology. This institution, compared with all major universities in the nation, is the special haven, it appears, of Catholic humanism.

The record of its baccalaureates is partly a result of the select quality of the students, partly a result of the requirements and emphases of the curriculum, and partly also the fact that graduates frequently enter clerical teaching orders requiring advanced degrees in the humanities. Its function as a leader in Catholic higher education suggests that the major Catholic contribution to American intellectual life in coming decades will probably be in the humanities.

Yale

Of all institutions reviewed in this study, Yale has probably been historically the most consistently hospitable to the humanities, if one excepts the special case of Catholic University. There is little point in presenting a detailed history of Yale. That Yale has been in the vanguard of American higher education since early colonial times is common knowledge. That it was the first American university to grant a doctorate is less well known. Some of the more recent aspects of Yale history, too, bear reviewing. It is commonly said that Yale first expanded from a college to a university during the administration of Dr. Angell. This is probably true, for before his time graduate study was spotty, scholarship was uneven, and the main focus of the institution was on its undergraduate program. Even before Angell, however, Yale was among the top six in the granting of doctorates.

The sciences had a special role and peculiar destiny at Yale. From the time of the Civil War until 1932, they were incorporated in the Sheffield Scientific School, a department of the university under more or less autonomous control, and looked upon with considerable contempt by the other sections of the university. Its low status was due to Sheffield's three-year degree, its geographical removal from the center of the Yale campus, its less rigorously enforced academic standards (including language requirements), and the fact that Sheffield students were regarded as largely ineligible for the higher social and scholastic honors offered to undergraduates. The Sheffield Scientific School persisted in its three-year program leading to the Ph.B. (Bachelor of Philosophy) degree until 1932, after which a four-year program was offered with more extensive humanities requirements. Finally, however, the Sheffield Scientific School abandoned undergraduate instruction entirely in 1946. This peculiar development in the history of Yale finds no parallel in other major eastern institutions, and accounts in part for the special ascendancy here of the humanities. A recent unpublished study has observed that even now the sciences are able to hold comparatively few of the undergraduates who come to Yale. Thus, in recent classes, the natural sciences claim only a tenth or less as majors upon graduation, although almost three times this number indicate scientific interests upon entrance. This report gives evidence that this is largely the result of the special intellectual and social climate of Yale, which places a premium on the humanities and social sciences at the expense of the natural sciences. At the present time approximately 40 per cent of their undergraduate student body major in the humanities.

Yale occupies a conspicuous position among those institutions that constitute the first factorial type as reported in Chapter 2. This class of Ivy League institutions produces a relatively high number of humanistic scholars from among their baccalaureates. Physical sciences, as distinct from the technologies, also show a superior record. Degrees in education, however, are few. Yale's record in the humanities is given in Table 58.

TABLE 58. Baccalaureate graduates of Yale who
continued to a Ph.D. in humanities.

B.A. Year		Foreign Languages	History	English	Fine Arts and Music	Philosophy	Total
Before	M	4	6	2	—	—	12
1926	F	—	—	—	—	—	—
1926-35	M	15	24	19	3	1	82
	F	—	—	—	1	—	1
1936-45	M	24	36	39	9	6	114
	F	1	—	—	—	—	1
1946-59	M	34	43	31	14	11	133
	F	—	—	—	—	—	—

The table makes clear that Yale's production of humanistic scholars is solid and sustained in all fields under consideration. The reader should be reminded that the figures for the final period cover those receiving baccalaureate degrees during 1946-59. Since the median time between

*,he B.A. and the Ph.D. is approximately eight years, it is clear that these figures do not represent the final number of persons taking the humanistic doctorate from these baccalaureate years. In fact, the final figures should inevitably be almost doubled.

In comparison with Harvard's record, as we shall see, Yale's is somewhat less impressive, for two reasons. First, it appears that Harvard's record of undergraduate recruitment to the humanities extends more surely into earlier decades; second, in the particular fields of fine arts and philosophy, Harvard's record is more voluminous and continuous. But it should be noted that the absence of undergraduate recruitment in the fine arts is now being remedied. Then, too, Yale has recently attained a superior position in languages.

The ratio of scientists to humanists among the 1936-56 graduates who have subsequently taken doctorates proves to be 1.5, a figure that is characteristically low and places Yale in company with other Ivy League institutions and among the lowest dozen of our most productive ninety-five institutions.

The output of Ph.D.'s granted by Yale in recent years, as taken from the National Academy of Sciences data, is given in Table 59.

TABLE 59. Ph.D. degrees granted by Yale.

Ph.D. Year	Physical Sciences	Biological Sciences	Social Sciences	Humanities	Education	Other
1936-42	194	124	117	245	79	79
1943-49	178	68	90	157	53	73
1950-56	395	157	199	374	91	144
TOTAL	767	349	406	776	223	296

Compared with other institutions, there is a heavy predominance of doctorates in the humanities. The ratio of Ph.D.'s in science to those in humanities, as we saw earlier, is low, standing at 1.4, approximating the ratio for undergraduates who continue to the doctorate and all in all yielding an entirely consistent picture. An examination of the record of doctorates in the humanities, as shown in Table 60, indicates that there has been a general and conspicuous increase in the most recently reported period of Yale's history. This increase in Ph.D. production is most marked in the fields of philosophy, languages, and probably fine arts, while history and English continue at a high rate of production already earlier established.

TABLE 60. Ph.D. degrees in humanities granted by Yale.

Ph.D. Year	Foreign Languages	History	English	Fine Arts and Music	Philosophy	Total
1936-42	59	63	106	4	13	245
1943-49	33	28	80	12	4	157
1950-56	113	84	110	18	49	374
TOTAL	205	175	296	34	66	776

An examination of the recruitment pattern of doctoral candidates for this institution is revealing. Seventy per cent of Yale Ph.D.'s who received their A.B. after 1946 and their Ph.D. before 1959 took the earlier degree in New England and the Mid-Atlantic states. Over a quarter of them are Yale undergraduates. Only a fifth are graduates of publicly supported institutions. This is entirely typical of Ivy League universities. The "provincialism" of this recruitment pattern is virtually duplicated in the case of Harvard, the other major Ivy League university observed by the writer. Finally, note should be taken that the lag time obtaining in the humanities at Yale is comparatively short, slightly over eight years on the average. Thus Yale like other Ivy League universities has a shorter time path to the doctorate than an average major university in the United States.

A complete review and evaluation of particular departments in the humanities is beyond the scope of this report. A few comments are in order, however. First, one must note the rise of fine arts at Yale in the past three decades, and its present expansion both as a field of research and as a physical institution. Thus, the fine art collection, which amounted to little until the 1930's, now is one of the most important in the nation, and Yale ranks with Harvard, Princeton, and NYU as one of the four centers of scholarship in this field. Philosophy, which in earlier years appeared to lag behind other departments, seems, since the war, to have taken on new life; this phenomenon seems to be connected with the department's shift in emphasis from classical philosophical inquiry to newer studies in logic and related fields. The languages at Yale appear to have a particularly vigorous group of representatives on the faculty. The history and English departments continue a long tradition of high effectiveness.

Leaving the problem of particular departments aside, there are a number of factors in the Yale picture that are more general in character and deserve expanded discussion. Among these is the quality of its facilities, as represented by the Sterling Library and by the fine arts collection housed in its museum. As one of the deans observed, such facilities are incapable of transportation and duplication as scientific equipment might be; therefore, one reason for the ascendancy of the humanities in the wealthier Ivy League institutions lies in their possession of these exceptional resources for humanistic study. Thus, for example, it is impossible to duplicate the Goethe collection in Yale's Sterling Library.

Another general factor that has strengthened the humanities at Yale is the kind of administrative control that has prevailed throughout its history. Yale has never had as a president a "practical" man, committed to the ideals of utility and service as are so many of the presidents of large state universities. Further, none have been scientists, unless Angell by some stretch of the imagination might be so classified. An examination of Yale's principal administrative officers and deans has shown only one in the sciences in recent years, whereas the humanities claim a substantial number. Further, as one dean pointed out, the humanists tend to have their offices located in the residence colleges whereas the scientists are tied to their laboratories and removed from the same degree of direct contact with students. It is almost literally true in a geographic sense to say that the humanities hold the center of the institution while the scientists reside on the periphery. And, finally, the masters of the houses are most frequently drawn from the humanities and social sciences.

It was a frequent comment at Yale that the position of the humanities there was in good part a matter of the tradition of serious and effective undergraduate teaching in the humanities in contrast to perfunctory teaching in the sciences. While the truth of this assertion can hardly be conclusively determined, still there is presumptive evidence in support of it. First, of course, is the aforementioned tendency toward physical alienation of the science faculty from the undergraduate student body. Beyond this, however, there is a long local tradition of the great, colorful teacher in the humanities, especially in English and history.

Still another factor, somewhat elusive in character but undoubtedly important, has been the quality and character of the Yale student body. One classicist explained the position of the humanities at Yale by the assertion "It is purely a matter of our clientele." He went on to observe that the Yale student body is or at least has been recruited from the eastern seaboard and from homes of superior educational standards and resources. For such students the humanities were not conceived as useless adornments, but rather as the pathway to urbanity, sophistication, and indeed successful careers in higher management and public affairs. This conviction that the committment of the Yale undergraduate to the humanities is greatly dictated by the regional and class origins of the student body possesses real plausibility, especially when one compares the "fashionable" fields of "majoring" at Yale with those in midwestern state institutions. It is reported that during the 1920's and 1930's well over 40 per cent of the undergraduates majored in English or history, and according to a recent study "majoring" in the sciences at Yale still has low prestige, especially from a social point of view.

There are, and have been, curricular features that are to the advantage of the humanities at Yale and that do not exist in other, especially state-supported, institutions. Thus, for example, the requirement in classical languages was maintained until the late 1930's, and an elective program in "directed studies" with emphasis on philosophy has been in effect for almost three decades. Study of basic courses in English, history, and modern languages for all students has been fairly vigorously enforced down to the present time. Even more striking is the absence of competing vocational curriculums, so dominant in publicly supported institutions. The curriculum is not designed to be "useful" or of "service" over the short term.

Within this context, one of my Yale informants presented what he felt were four obstacles to the development of a high order of scholarship, especially in the humanities, at state universities. I shall report them here, not because I consider them unassailable but because they will provide useful hypotheses in my subsequent review of state universities. These four barriers to high scholastic excellence, as he saw them, were (1) a short-sighted dedication to service and utility as educational objectives, establishing an educational climate emphasizing the practical and vocational over the intellectual and theoretical; (2) an immediacy of political and fiscal control by relatively incompetent persons selected from state governments and legislatures; (3) the general inability or unwillingness to enforce a high degree of selectiveness in the admissions of students, making for lowered standards of instruction and attainment; and (4) the quality of depersonalization and anonymity attendant upon huge numbers, pervasive bureaucratization, and "mass-production" theory of education.

Let us summarize what may be generally said to account for the particular eminence of the humanities at Yale. Probably first is the simple fact that Yale began and was dominated throughout most of its history by humanistic disciplines. This pattern continues today. The sciences, technologies, and professional schools were later grafted onto the humanistic disciplines, with the sciences placed under a special disadvantage in the Sheffield Scientific School. Again, the leadership of Yale, from the presidency through the higher administrative staff and to the heads of the houses, has been heavily selected from among humanistic scholars. This has been accompanied by a disavowal of vocational educational aims and curriculums. Further, there has been a long and vigorous tradition of colorful undergraduate teaching in the humanities that does not find its parallel in the sciences. Also, the regional and cultural selection of the student body has made for a disinterest in "vocational" education and a receptiveness to the arts and humanities with which social, personal, and political status has been associated. These areas of study provide that kind of instruction in style and taste that has commanded a premium in the Yale "culture." Finally, there is the fact that the curriculum gives more than usual support and deference to the humanities.

Harvard

Harvard ranks second in recent years only to Columbia in the production of Ph.D.'s in the humanities, and many scholars would place it unconditionally first with respect to quality. Thus the eminence of Harvard in the humanities is beyond dispute. And like Yale, its distinction in the sciences, while outstanding both in respect to quality and to numbers, still is less than that in the humanities, a pattern identified earlier in the factor analytic study as characteristic of Ivy League institutions.

I shall not here attempt any lengthy historical sketch of the emergence of Harvard. But it should be noted that there are some striking parallels with Yale, with which Harvard is naturally linked in this study. Both date to early colonial times; both remained under the aegis of Congregationalism until the nineteenth century. Both Yale and Harvard early became recognized centers of scholarship and were first and third, respectively, among American institutions of higher learning in the granting of doctorates. Both have in the main avoided vocational training, at least at the undergraduate level, emphasized humanities over the sciences, fostered college or house plans, attracted the wealthy and the endowed, and become symbols of social and intellectual aristocracy. Still it would be misleading to conclude that Harvard and Yale have not had some significant differences in their development. First, I think, the sciences have had a happier fate at Harvard than at Yale; not merely because they were never separated into a special school of inferior status, but also because there were abler spokesmen, both on the faculty and in the administration, for science at Harvard. Again, Harvard had a longer and more impressive history of scientific attainment than Yale, despite the latter's early claim to such men as the physicist Willard Gibbs. Certainly in this century, with Eliot and his progressive scientific interests and subsequently with Conant, Harvard seems to have received science with more cordiality. But this difference is clearly a difference of degree.

Whereas Yale granted the first Ph.D. in America, Harvard shortly superseded her in graduate scholarship and has maintained a significant lead numerically in most fields since the nineteenth century. Thus, a secure tradition of graduate scholarship appears to have been established at Harvard before Yale and in some areas, notably fine arts and philosophy, Harvard's record is more continuous. Further, while Yale remained committed to a fixed classical curriculum until the 1930's, Harvard very early in the regime of Eliot inaugurated the free, or comparatively free, elective system. Somehow it appears that in a number of respects Harvard was more ready to experiment with educational ventures than Yale and that a more conservative tone has and does prevail at the latter.

The similarities and not the differences between the undergraduate student bodies of the two institutions is clearly most striking. Both have historically drawn their students from the Northeast and from homes with both financial comfort and educational traditions. In recent times, especially since the war, certain changes have occurred in both institutions affecting their student clientele. These changes result from the increase of the undergraduate body, the extensive program of scholarship aid, allegedly greater at Harvard than at Yale, and from the changed criteria for admission. During the depression years at Harvard, approximately 75 per cent of all applicants were accepted, the essential qualifications being literacy and the capacity to pay one's bills. Presumably such a condition obtained at Yale, though figures of this period are not available.

Since World War II and ever increasingly as time lapses, the criterion of admission has been not financial but scholastic. Thus the community tone of both institutions has undergone a change in the past two or three decades, though this would be easy to overestimate. In both institutions, as we have seen in the discussion of Yale, there remains a marked tendency to the special cultivation of, and respect for, humanistic disciplines. Indeed, this institutional climate appears to be effective in both institutions, luring prospective scientists (undergraduates) from their proposed field to the social sciences and humanities. Finally, it is perhaps worth noting that if the climate of Yale has been traditionally more conservative than that at Harvard, in educational as well as religious and political matters, this is reflected too in the careers sought and attained by its alumni. Thus, Yale men, according to a current study, more commonly succeed in higher industrial management and Harvard men in scholarship and governmental service. Both, however, contribute vastly to each of these domains.

Harvard is easily the single institution most productive of baccalaureate graduates who continue to the doctorate in the humanities. It holds this position over its nearest competitor, California (Berkeley), by a margin of 40 per cent, and is greater in all four periods under consideration. The special eminence of Harvard further extends to virtually all humanistic fields under consideration. In Period IV it yields first position to Yale in foreign languages and literature and to Chicago in philosophy. But in both instances it places second in absolute numbers. In Period III it yields to other institutions only in philosophy and in arts and music. Other fields of scholarship are not neglected; in fact it places tenth in the sciences in Periods III and IV combined. But the eminence of Harvard in the humanities is virtually uncontested.

Table 61 shows the number of persons taking their B.A. from Harvard in different time intervals who are listed in the roster of our humanistic scholars receiving their doctorates during 1936-1959. That this is a particularly solid record may be seen by comparing this table with those prepared for other major institutions reviewed in this study. One must also be mindful that this record, which reports absolute numbers, comes from an institution with a relatively small number of graduates. The average annual graduating class at Harvard for

Period III was a little over eight hundred and for our Period IV approximately twelve hundred. In each period I reckon the rate at which its graduates continue to the doctorate in the humanities at approximately 1 in 40, or 2.5 per cent, a remarkably high figure.

TABLE 61. Baccalaureate graduates of Harvard who continued to a Ph.D. in humanities.

B.A. Year		Foreign Languages	History	English	Fine Arts and Music	Philosophy	Total
Before	M	9	14	7	3	3	36
1926	F	—	—	—	—	—	—
1926-35	M	37	38	31	11	10	127
	F	—	—	—	—	—	—
1936-45	M	47	64	51	19	16	197
	F	—	—	—	—	—	—
1946-59	M	30	61	58	15	17	181
	F	—	—	—	—	—	—

It is to be expected for several reasons that the ratio of those continuing in science to those continuing in humanities would be low. This is indeed so, the ratio standing at 1.6, very slightly exceeding that at Yale, but far below the figure characteristic of state universities.

In the actual granting of doctoral degrees in the humanities Harvard again has a special eminence, standing second only to Columbia in point of numbers from 1936 to 1956, and surely not below that institution in reputation for quality. Here again, as among the baccalaureate graduates, the ratio of those in science to those in the humanities is quite low, namely 1.2, placing Harvard third among all major universities, after Catholic University and Columbia. Table 62 shows in more detail the pattern of doctorates granted in recent times in all areas of scholarship at Harvard.

The record of the numbers and fields of humanistic doctorates

TABLE 62. Ph.D. degress granted by Harvard.

Ph.D. Year	Physical Sciences	Biological Sciences	Social Sciences	Humanities	Education	Other
1936-42	234	135	231	334	4	29
1943-49	263	76	256	253	36	44
1950-56	538	183	644	584	171	144
TOTAL	1035	394	1131	1171	211	217

granted by Harvard in recent times is shown in Table 63. The table deserves comment only because of the sustained balance and impressive numbers involved. Harvard's record is particularly strong in fine arts and in history, whereas in comparison with Yale it is relatively weak in foreign languages. But these are minor observations upon a remarkably solid and sustained output of humanistic scholars.

TABLE 63. Ph.D. degrees in humanities granted
by Harvard.

Ph.D. Year	Foreign Languages	History	English	Fine Arts and Music	Philosophy	Total
1936-42	89	110	79	27	29	334
1943-49	40	84	68	26	35	253
1950-56	105	214	167	53	45	584
TOTAL	234	408	314	106	109	1171

It is interesting to observe that despite its international reputation Harvard shows the same kind of provincialism in its selection of graduate students in the humanities that we have remarked in other institutions. Thus, we find over 50 per cent are selected from New England institutions and over 70 per cent from the Northeast. Only 17 per cent are graduates of publicly supported institutions while almost 80 per cent come from nonsectarian and Protestant colleges. Just under 30 per cent are baccalaureates from Harvard itself.

How long does it take between one's baccalaureate degree and his Harvard doctorate? The figures show that the lapsed time is only slightly longer than at Yale: 9.7 years, on the average. This is a relatively fast course compared to other institutions, especially most state universities.

What factors have augured for the special enthronement of the humanities at Harvard? I should probably begin with the simple observation that, as at Yale and most other Ivy League institutions, the humanities constituted the initial focus of the institution; only in the latter part of the nineteenth century were the sciences and social sciences added. Beyond this, it is clear that Harvard has not been hospitable to the short-term educational aims emphasizing vocation and utility. Harvard does, to be sure, have a school of engineering, but it is relatively obscure. On the other hand, special note should be taken of the extraordinary facilities for the humanistic scholar available at Harvard. Most important are the facilities of Widener Library, which in English literature, history, and languages are second to none save the Library of Congress. The Fogg Art Museum is one of the most important in the nation, and in the field of fine arts Harvard is especially noted for its training of museum administrators.

As noted before, the humanities are frequently more bound to bibliographic and material resources than the sciences, which depend on relatively mobile or easily duplicated equipment. One must in most cases be actually present at one of the four or five great libraries in order to pursue the highest quality of humanistic scholarship. The sciences, on the other hand, can generally be transported as equipment is transported, though it must be admitted that certain scientific fields, for example nuclear physics, are becoming immobilized and fixed to expensive installations. The implications of this difference for the extension of scholarship in both the humanities and sciences are central to any future projections of scholarly endeavor.

Many of the observations concerning the intellectual climate at Yale apply also at Harvard, at least throughout the main part of its history. Here humanities have been considered not useless and effeminate but rather a mark of culture and of membership in a privileged class. As at Yale, the study of the humanities has been a vocational advantage, not a disadvantage, to those entering the world of business or public affairs. Though two of Harvard's recent presidents were in fact affiliated with the sciences, its most potent administrative figures have been drawn from the social sciences and the humanities, and even their scientist presidents were in no sense men of practical or utilitarian bent. It is no real coincidence that at the present time all but one of the houses at Harvard is presided over by humanists or social scientists. These men occupy a very special office beyond that of administrators. In a very real sense they are the arbiters of style and taste in thought and attitude, and their influence on the undergraduate is powerful and direct.

At least two of my informants at Harvard made particular mention of the degree to which the Harvard faculty finds it leadership and its most eloquent spokesmen in the ranks of the humanists. They insisted that the proceedings of a Harvard faculty meeting place a premium upon the kind of style and eloquence of persuasion that is the prov-

ince of those humanistically trained. So, just as the houses are dominated by humanistic masters in the main, the faculty is led by men of
humanistic commitment.

As one observer, who has been on the Harvard faculty for a decade
or more after serving in a midwestern state university, put it, the entire fabric of Harvard, and Ivy League institutions generally, is dominated by a kind of logic of finesse as distinct from the logic of geome-
try, to borrow Pascal's famous distinction. Thus, tables of organiza-
tion and chains of command mean comparatively little in institutions
like Harvard, whose bureaucratic structure has all manner of hidden
avenues, and whose leadership reposes more in men and their per-
suasiveness rather than the formal recognition of office and seniority.
This observation, which surely has some validity, appears to me to
apply equally well to Yale.

Any summary of the factors that promote the distinction of Harvard in the humanities necessarily repeats in good measure those cited
in the instance of Yale. The similarities of the two institutions are far
greater than the differences that we have noted in passing. As in the
case of Yale, we observe that there is an administrative disdain for
utilitarian and service educational aims, and that the sciences and
technologies were the *parvenus* and not the founders of the institution.
Beyond this, the special student clientele of Harvard has been drawn
historically from educated classes, who in turn became the alumni
who zealously support the humanistic tradition. Finally, there are the
unique facilities offered by the Widener Library, the Fogg Art Museum, and other installations that render Harvard the possessor of
facilities for the highest order of humanistic scholarship. These un-
duplicated facilities attract the master scholar and teacher, who in turn
attract the most able students in substantial numbers. This condition is
not likely to be abruptly reversed.

TWO WESTERN UNIVERSITIES

In this chapter I shall report on two major universities of the West, the University of California at Berkeley and Stanford University. They pose an interesting contrast between one of the most advanced state universities and the nearest thing to an Ivy League university located west of the Mississippi. But in many respects each is unique. Berkeley, as we shall see, is by no means typical of state institutions but represents a most fortunate and advanced development of that type. Stanford, on the other hand, has many features that remove it from major private eastern universities. Together, however, they constitute the two most important universities west of the Mississippi, occupy the same region, share many traditions, and provide an interesting study in similarities and contrasts.

California (Berkeley)

The higher educational system of California is one of the most elaborate and complicated in the nation, and it enrolls more students than any other state system. At the pinnacle of this structure stands the University of California at Berkeley, which in many respects is the most envied state university in the nation. It is probably the only state university that can compete on equal and sometimes advantageous terms for top scholars with the major Ivy League universities. Administrators and professors in midwestern and other state universities look to Berkeley as an institution upon which they hope to model themselves, and regard it as a precedent-establishing vanguard among publicly supported institutions.

The situation of Berkeley can only be understood in terms of the total structure of higher education in California. This system begins at the lowest level with a system of junior colleges that serves the undergraduate community needs throughout the state for the first two years. Next in the hierarchy, at least historically, has been the state college system, comprising some fifteen four-year colleges, which, until very recently, have been controlled by the State Board of Education. Beyond this is the university system, with its several branches, in Los Angeles, Santa Barbara, Davis, and Berkeley. Of these various branches, that in Berkeley, and second to it that in Los Angeles, has been the most important in point of scholarship. The existence of this hierarchical structure has made it possible to create in Berkeley a special dedication to quality with respect to student admissions, research support, and light teaching loads that few state universities have been privileged to attain and that is in many respects reminiscent of the Ivy League universities.

It will be recalled that I have had occasion to present four considerations advanced by one of my informants at Yale, which, in his judgment, represented institutional liabilities of publicly supported institutions in America in their pursuit of the highest order of scholarly eminence, especially within the humanities. It is illuminating to examine the degree to which they are applicable or inapplicable to Berkeley.

Berkeley seems to have evaded the first force that, according to our Eastern informant, has doomed the state university to mediocrity. I refer here to the alleged dedication to service and utilitarianism. To a considerable extent, Berkeley has escaped this fate partly because its graduate program is so heavily featured, partly because of the quality of students and their more scholarly dedication, and partly because service and utilitarian functions in higher education have been allocated to other branches of the state university system, the college system, and even the junior college system. These functions are, so to speak, farmed out, leaving the Berkeley campus to address itself primarily to the basic arts and sciences, though, to be sure, there are an engineering school, a graduate school of business administration, and a school of education.

The second indictment was the directness of political control by agencies of the state government. Berkeley, unlike many state institutions, is relatively immune to the whims of legislative action by the state government. This condition comes about for several reasons. First, the university system is governed by a body of regents, sixteen of whom are appointed for a term of sixteen years. The board members are not subject to ready removal, and their office is considered one of the highest public dignities that can be bestowed by the state, comparable in all respects to appointment to the State Supreme Court. A second limitation on political control is financial. Less than half of the operating budget of Berkeley comes from legislative appropriation, while more than half comes from federal contracts and from the income from its impressive private endowment. Beyond this, its budget is not subject to detailed item review by the legislature but is granted in terms of an over-all appropriation, whose particular allocation is subject to the decision of the university administration and Board of Regents. Thus Berkeley has attained, compared with most public universities, a peculiar freedom from legislative control by technically incompetent persons.

The third indictment of state institutions was directed toward their obligation to accept for admission virtually all state high school graduates. Berkeley has succeeded within the context of the larger state system in maintaining a high degree of exclusiveness with respect to both graduate and undergraduate admissions. At the present time, it is maintained that the undergraduate student body is selected from the upper 15 per cent of high school graduates throughout the state, while out-of-state applicants are selected even more severely. The graduate students, numbering approximately 8,000 in all fields, also are selected by high standards in comparison with admissions standards in most state universities. It should also be observed that of the total student body at Berkeley the undergraduates number approximately 12,000. Thus, graduate instruction is clearly a major focus of this institution, while the undergraduate student body represents, relatively speaking, an intellectual elite with strong scholarly leanings. Berkeley has succeeded beyond any other publicly supported institution in eliminating the great burden of uninspired and unendowed students that encumber so many public institutions.

Finally, it was alleged that the state university, by its sheer undifferentiated mass, begot a kind of anonymous facelessness among its students, and that this quality was hostile to the development of serious scholarship, especially in the humanities. This charge cannot be so readily answered as the other three in the case of Berkeley, though it is probably the least weighty of the four indictments. Examining the undergraduate program at Berkeley, we do find classes large, undergraduate instruction in the main impersonal, and the turnover of students from year to year, transferring in and out, substantial. The fraternity and sorority systems provide a community identification for only a small fraction of the undergraduate body. Compared with most Ivy League institutions, it is probable that the sense of student identity is less fostered here.

Let us now examine the record of Berkeley, first, with respect to its pattern in the undergraduate production of those who go on to a doctorate. As the results presented in Chapter 2 show, Berkeley is not a "pure" type for though it is to be predominantly identified with state and land grant institutions, still it shows a substantial participation in the so-called Ivy League factor at the same time that it is strong in the physical sciences and technology. It appears in some respects, therefore, to have escaped the "grassroots" commitment of the typical state (and especially land grant) institution.

Its record in the production of humanists from among its baccalaureates is very impressive. It stands second, after Harvard, among all institutions in Period III, and third, after Harvard and Yale, in Period IV. By a very comfortable margin, it exceeds numerically all other publicly supported institutions. Thus, Berkeley is to be included with the major Ivy League institutions as a foremost baccalaureate source of humanistic scholars, though it must be recognized that its undergraduate student body is substantially greater. This state of affairs is of course reflected in the relatively low male indices of humanistic scholarship for Berkeley, 7.0 for Period III and 9.1 for Period IV.

Table 64 shows the numbers of baccalaureates who have continued in different fields of humanities to a doctorate in the four periods. In the first place, we may note the rather special ascendancy of the history department as compared with the other humanistic disciplines, a characteristic that is shared even more strikingly by Stanford. There is a clear suggestion in these data that, of all the disciplines considered here, history is the most evenly and widely distributed geographically and suffers least from an undue concentration in a select class of eastern institutions. A second thing of note is the relative paucity of contributions in the fine arts as compared with Ivy League institutions. Here we are immediately made aware of the fact that frontier regions, including the West, have been at a serious disadvantage in developing the fine arts in their universities by virtue of the concentration of bibliographic and museum resources along the eastern seaboard. The contribution of women to the record of Berkeley is substantial. In fact, in the first period there are 18 female graduates who continued to the doctorate in the years covered by our record, a figure considerably exceeding the number of men in this period. This may in part be a

statistical artifact, but it does point up the fact that a meaningful
number of women graduates from Berkeley have continued to a
scholarly career in the humanities.

TABLE 64. Baccalaureate graduates of Berkeley who
continued to a Ph.D. in humanities.

B.A. Year		Foreign Languages and Literature	History	English	Fine Arts and Music	Philosophy	Total
Before	M	3	3	3	1	—	10
1926	F	6	5	4	—	3	18
1926-35	M	21	26	13	5	6	71
	F	5	1	1	—	4	11
1936-45	M	20	59	24	3	12	118
	F	5	5	2	1	1	14
1946-59	M	29	38	29	4	6	106
	F	1	—	1	1	—	3

Let us now consider the all-important ratios relating humanities to
science. At Berkeley, for baccalaureates, this ratio stands at 4.6. It will
be recalled that the figures for Harvard and Yale were 1.6 and 1.5
respectively. It is clear that in dealing with Berkeley, we are considering an institution that harbors a significantly different intellectual climate, in which the sciences, physical and biological, apparently command a far greater proportion of the scholarly talent. This ratio of 4.6
is typical of state universities in general, though it is lower than many,
especially those founded under the Morrill Act.

Turning now to the graduate record, we may observe in Table 65
that, according to the figures compiled by the National Academy of
Sciences, Berkeley granted 551 Ph.D.'s in the humanities between
1936 and 1956, while the figures for the social sciences (excluding
history) stand at 559. Compared with these, almost 2,200 Ph.D.'s
were granted in the physical and biological sciences, that is, four times
as many as in the humanities and twice as many as in the humanities
and social sciences combined. In terms of the numbers of doctorates
granted, the science-humanities ratio is approximately 4.0, consistent
with the figure obtained from a consideration of baccalaureate production and unlike comparable ratios obtained for Ivy League institutions. Moreover, the advantage of the sciences over the humanities
appears to have increased in the most recent time period reported in
the table.

TABLE 65. Ph.D. degrees granted by Berkeley.

Ph.D. Year	Physical Sciences	Biological Sciences	Social Sciences	Humanities	Education	Other
1936-42	227	231	104	166	53	3
1943-49	235	229	89	128	74	1
1950-56	743	520	366	257	187	5
TOTAL	1205	980	559	551	314	9

Table 66 shows the number of doctorates granted by Berkeley by the several humanities departments during recent time intervals. Four observations are worth making: first, the vigor of the history department; second, the sustained quality of the record over two decades; third, the comparative weakness of the arts and music; and finally, the notable record of the philosophy department, a rarity among state institutions and institutions of the West. These parallel directly our observations of the baccalaureate record.

TABLE 66. Ph.D. degrees in humanities granted by Berkeley.

Ph.D. Year	Foreign Languages	History	English	Fine Arts and Music	Philosophy	Total
1936-42	40	75	34	—	17	166
1943-49	30	61	23	1	13	128
1950-56	64	114	58	4	17	257
TOTAL	134	250	115	5	47	551

The recruitment of graduate students in the humanities at Berkeley offers occasion for special comment. We are dealing here with the origins of persons receiving their baccalaureate degree in 1946 or thereafter who have since obtained a doctorate in the humanities at Berkeley. To begin with, the startling regionalism of Berkeley is manifest in the fact that 62 per cent of the humanities doctorates took their B.A. on the Pacific Coast, while 45 per cent were actually B.A.'s from Berkeley itself. Again, 67 per cent had taken their baccalaureate degrees from publicly supported institutions, while only 28 per cent had attended private institutions. These figures are radically different from those for the Ivy League institutions, and reflect partly the difference in regional style of higher education. They also illustrate the educational provincialism that has been discussed earlier in connection with humanistic education in America in general.

Finally, a brief comment should be made concerning the lapsed time between baccalaureate and doctoral degrees for graduate students at Berkeley. On the basis of data obtained from the National Academy of Sciences the mean figure stands at 10.3 years for men and 11.9 years for women as earlier reported. Berkeley therefore provides a fast pathway to the Ph.D. when compared with most public institutions, but slower than for Ivy League institutions.

It is evident from the foregoing record that Berkeley stands at the very summit of the state universities in the nation by almost any scholarly standard. Berkeley's record in the fields of history, English, and foreign languages is solid and continuous for several decades. Its record in the fine arts is relatively weak as compared with high-quality private eastern institutions. In the case of the fine arts there is the simple problem of facilities. The present music building has been in service less than a decade, while the fine arts department still lacks a major center. The music school does indeed possess a superior collection of musical manuscripts for scholarly study. It has also recently instituted a plan for the granting of doctorates in composition, a rising trend among state universities but not among the major universities of the eastern seaboard. We shall have occasion elsewhere to discuss this difference in educational philosophy in the fine arts. It is probably no coincidence that history established itself at Berkeley so vigorously and that the fine arts lagged comparatively. This is indeed to be predicted, given the frontier ethos of the region and the degree to which it has tended to undervalue the contemplative and the aesthetic.

In the end we must ask how Berkeley has attained its pre-eminent position among state universities in the training of humanists. Let us sum up some of the major facts. Partly it has attained this position by force of numbers since it is one of our largest state universities, especially in its graduate department. Probably of equal importance, however, is the fact that at both graduate and undergraduate levels Berkeley has been able to maintain a degree of student selectivity unrealized in any other public institution in the nation. As we have noted, this is possible, given the special terms of its incorporation and the existence of many other facets of the Californian system of higher education. We have also noted that Berkeley has been able for various reasons to resist the obligation to immediate service and to utilitarian educational aims in favor of more scholarly ideals. This, in large part, stems from the school's relative financial independence and from the organizational cushions that protect it from direct legislative coercion. Added to these are other considerations: the concentration of a self-appointed intelligentsia among the Berkeley student body and in neighboring regions, and a curriculum that has, in recent years, maintained substantial requirements in the humanities. The result of all this is a unique institution, with a distinguished record in the production of humanists both from its undergraduate and graduate student bodies, at the same time that the physical and biological sciences attain an even greater eminence.

Stanford

Many persons not closely acquainted with the history and character of Stanford University would identify it as the "Princeton of the West" —the western outpost of the Ivy League institutions—but such an image requires multiple and careful qualifications. Stanford, in the end, is a university quite of its own stamp, a curious mixture of the aristocratic eastern university, the frontier technological institution, and the institution dedicated to public service. Moreover, unlike major Ivy League universities, it is coeducational and does not possess the venerable history attaching to Harvard, Yale, and Princeton. It is, in short, a puzzling institution, *sui generis,* that defies quick and facile classification.

Stanford began as a monument to Leland Stanford Jr., whose father was senator from California and a multimillionaire by virtue of wealth accumulated in the Southern Pacific Railway. The university was established in the late 1880's with an endowment reckoned at twenty million dollars or slightly more, placing it ahead of Harvard, Yale, and all other institutions in the nation in financial resources. From the first, it had strong technological and practical leanings so that mining and engineering, and presently a School of Medicine and a School of Law, were assigned primary emphasis. Beyond this, it was not conceived of as a school for the wealthy; during the first few years no tuition whatsoever was required, and thereafter, for a number of years, only very nominal charges. It is probably fair to observe that the humanities were not particularly emphasized here. In fact, in contrast to the Ivy League, their development has been appended to a curricular emphasis that is technological and professional.

What has been the pattern of Stanford's general history over seven decades? Up to the 1930's it increased in size as its endowment, invested in railway bonds and stocks, became increasingly depreciated. Women continued to be admitted but in relatively small numbers, based on an early quota. A very powerful constellation of professional schools developed at Stanford; the humanities were not able to compete effectively with them for positions of power or for financial support and resources. A very significant development occurred, however, through the gifts of Herbert Hoover, particularly with the establishment of the Hoover Library collection. This brought concern with political affairs and history to special prominence, which, as we shall presently see, is reflected in the record of Stanford graduates and Stanford doctorates.

Stanford differs from the Ivy League institutions in its type of leadership. The first president of Stanford was David Starr Jordan, who went there after a basic education and indoctrination at Cornell, a varied career as Professor of Natural History and Biology, and a period as President of Indiana University. He, like two of his successors, Wilbur and Tressider, was a medical doctor. It is said that Jordan shaped the early Stanford much in the image of Cornell; Cornell, it will be recalled, had a private university's core to which a number of professional and technical schools supported by state funds were appended. The considerable strength assigned to these professional schools at Stanford finds its precedent, therefore, at Cornell. The second president, Branner, held fairly brief tenure, mostly during World War I, and was a geologist by training. The third president, Ray Lyman Wilbur, had a very long period of office from 1916 to 1943. He was an intimate of Herbert Hoover and took a leave of absence from Stanford to serve as Secretary of the Interior in his cabinet. He was also a medically trained man and sympathetic to the professional schools of Stanford. On the retirement of Wilbur in 1943 still another medical doctor, Donald B. Tressider, held the presidency until 1948, at which time he was succeeded by the present president, J. W. Wallace Sterling. Sterling is the first president in Stanford's history whose training has not been primarily in medicine, science, or technology; his field is political science and history. This pattern of presidential selection is more consonant with the traditions of technological schools than of Ivy League institutions.

Returning to some other aspects of Stanford's development, one finds that by the mid-1930's the endowment resources of the institution had sunk to a very low level, partly through mismanagement but mostly because of the peculiar conditions of their bestowal. The humanities seemed to suffer more from neglect than did the professional schools of law, engineering, medicine, mining, and education. Stanford's fine arts department achieved minimal development from a scholarly point of view, though a collection of Oriental art of some moment existed. The music department was devoted largely to ancillary instruction and the performing arts. It is perhaps characteristic that the most important museum is a medical museum. The bright spot in Stanford's development, then, was the above-mentioned Hoover Memorial Library.

Since World War II Stanford has emerged from a weakened and convalescent position to a robust status. In looking over the recent history of several departments, one is impressed with the fact that the field of history, tolerably well supported for several decades, has come to unusual vitality. The arts, on the other hand, have not attained anything like the emphasis accorded them at Ivy League institutions, while the Stanford departments of languages and English have suffered and probably still suffer from some neglect. In the languages, especially, there developed a custom of maintaining staff members at the assistant professor level, counting upon the attractions of the climate and sentimental commitments to bind them to their office.

The manner in which Stanford effected its recovery and brought itself to a position in which it might support the humanities commensurately with its professional schools requires a few comments. The current president, Dr. Sterling, with the trustees, established a policy of granting long-term leases of Stanford lands to selected industries of a highly technological sort, especially electronics. This has enabled Stanford to derive very substantial income from extensive property holdings that were previously unproductive. It has had the further advantage of bringing to the vicinity of the university a concentration of highly trained technologists and scientists, which inevitably influences the university. In addition to this, the university has established a research corporation whose services extend over the physical and biological sciences and into the fields of research in economics, psychology, and sociology. This, too, has had the effect of attracting researchers of a highly selective order. Approximately ten years ago Stanford was able to attract the Center for Advanced Studies in the Behavioral Sciences to its immediate vicinity and while Stanford has no direct connection with this Center, it unquestionably benefits by its proximity. Finally, it should be mentioned that Stanford has succeeded in obtaining a grant of twenty-five million dollars from the Ford Foundation on a very generous matching basis. All of these developments have conspired to lift Stanford in point of finance and prestige from the dark hours of the late 1930's to its proud position as the first private university west of the Appalachians, excepting possibly Chicago. The humanities in the main have still to realize the full benefits of this new affluence. At the present time, however, the Humanities Council at Stanford is pressing for greater financial support and, in particular, for the development of a fine arts center worthy of the institution.

Something should be said about the special qualities of the student body at Stanford. We have dwelt heretofore upon aspects of Stanford that distinguish it from the private Ivy League institutions of the East: the scientific training of its presidents, its late historical origins, its preferred support of technological and professional schools, and its singular financial history. Still, as we shall presently see, there are indeed points of similarity between Stanford and eastern Ivy League institutions, and these relate particularly to the pattern characterizing its undergraduates and its graduate students in their scholarly pursuits. Relatively, the humanities are preferred areas, more so for Stanford undergraduates than for those taking doctorates there. I suspect that this is related in a direct and important way to the fact that the humanities claim their adherents from individuals inheriting an educational tradition, while the vocational fields are likely to be selected by first generation college material. Certainly Stanford, like Ivy League institutions, has, apart from its earliest years and its most recent years, been an exclusive university of high cost and high social prestige, attracting the sons of the wealthy and the educated in much the same way as have our eastern private universities. Despite the avowed intent of the founders, Stanford has become the socially and intellectually prestigeful private university of the West without a single competitor on the horizon. As such it has attracted a special preselected clientele that I believe is especially hospitable to the humanities.

Examining the record of Stanford with respect to the scholarly careers pursued by its baccalaureates, one finds, as reported in Chapter 2, that it is primarily identified with the Ivy League humanistic pattern, and secondarily with the technological pattern. This is not too surprising considering, on the one hand, the quality of its clientele and, on the other, the attraction of its professional schools, especially in the physical sciences and technologies. In the humanites themselves we can see in Table 67 the number of those graduates who have continued to the doctorate in the five fields under consideration. This particular record offers some unusual features.

TABLE 67. Baccalaureate graduates of Stanford who continued to a Ph.D. in humanities.

B.A. Year		Foreign Languages	History	English	Fine Arts and Music	Philosophy	Total
Before	M	2	3	1	—	1	7
1926	F	2	1	1	1	—	5
1926-35	M	13	24	16	3	4	60
	F	1	2	4	—	—	7
1936-45	M	7	19	6	—	2	34
	F	1	2	3	—	2	8
1946-59	M	4	21	7	2	7	41
	F	—	1	—	—	—	1

First is the strength of the history department, which, in all periods and especially since 1936, has been particularly productive. Compared with this department, foreign languages and English are barren. Fine arts and music, as we might suspect, show a very small yield, even considering that they are relatively unpopular disciplines. Similarly, philosophy is undistinguished with the possible exception of the period since World War II.

A second thing of note concerning Stanford's baccalaureate record is the singularly high production among its baccalaureates from 1926 to 1935, followed by a sharp falling off in the next decade and a slight rise in the decade since World War II. This pattern appears in no other of the major institutions reviewed here and may perhaps be further confirmation of the interpretation that the fortunes, quality, and morale of Stanford underwent a sharp decline in the late 1930's and early 1940's.

It is illuminating again, however, to point out that the science-humanities ratio for baccalaureates, which has proved such a key index to the intellectual thrust of an institution, shows Stanford more akin to the Ivy League pattern than to that of most major state universities. Thus, this ratio stands at 2.3, substantially but not radically higher than Yale and Harvard. Still, it is far below such public institutions as Indiana, Wisconsin, Berkeley, and, above all, Ohio State, elsewhere reviewed.

Turning to the record of doctorates granted between 1936 and 1956, we find in Table 68 that the distinctive feature of Stanford's pattern is the very high number of degrees granted in education, a number closely approaching those given in the physical and biological sciences together. This is consistent with a picture of Stanford devoting large energies to its professional graduate schools, and sets it off from most Ivy League universities, excepting possibly Columbia. The ratio between doctorate degrees in science and those in humanities stands at 2.8, indicating that the graduate student body is somewhat more committed to the sciences than the baccalaureate graduates, a fact again consistent with our general evaluation. Still, this ratio is substantially below the majority of state universities.

TABLE 68. Ph.D. degrees granted by Stanford.

Ph.D. Year	Physical Sciences	Biological Sciences	Social Sciences	Humanities	Education	Other
1936-42	100	54	50	73	89	6
1943-49	123	56	43	52	223	11
1950-56	374	95	140	158	418	51
TOTAL	579	205	233	283	730	68

It should be observed in Table 69 that doctorates granted in the humanities since 1936 are heavily concentrated in the departments of history and English, as reported earlier. Notable is the absence of a sustained graduate tradition in philosophy and the arts. In the most recent period it will be observed that the English department has been particularly active.

If we consider graduate students in humanities at Stanford who have taken their baccalaureates since 1946, we find that slightly less than half of them come from institutions on the Pacific Coast, while one-fifth of them are graduates of Stanford itself. Interestingly enough, almost 35 per cent come from the Midwest and North Atlantic states.

TABLE 69. Ph.D. degrees in humanities granted by
Stanford.

Ph.D. Year	Foreign Languages	History	English	Fine Arts and Music	Philosophy	Total
1936-42	27	26	19	—	1	73
1943-49	16	24	12	—	—	52
1950-56	30	64	58	5	1	158
TOTAL	73	114	89	5	2	283

The South is scarcely represented at all. Despite the fact that Stanford
is located in the West where publicly supported institutions are numerically dominant, only 34 per cent of Stanford's graduate students in
the humanities come from publicly supported schools, while the remaining 66 per cent come from private, mostly nonsectarian, universities and colleges. This is in rather sharp contrast to neighboring Berkeley, where 67 per cent come from public institutions. This supports
the general hypothesis that institutions tend to select their graduate
students, at least in the humanities, from other institutions of the same
type and same region as themselves. In Stanford's case the commitment
to type, all things considered, seems more striking than the commitment to region.

One final note on graduate study in the humanities at Stanford is
contained in a consideration of the lag-time record. Stanford has one
of the greatest intervals between B.A. and Ph.D. in the humanities of
any major institution. The figures stand at 12.1 years for men and 11.9
years for women, though the latter figure is based on only a small number of cases and is probably not reliable. It was suggested to me that
one of the reasons for this long interval lies in the relatively poor
traditional support of the humanities at Stanford and the requirement
that virtually all graduate students pursue their program at half pace
or less while employed as departmental assistants. Whether this be true
or not, this is the highest figure reported for any of the institutions reviewed here.

Any summary of the evaluation of Stanford would have to take into
account the fact that Stanford fits no clear pattern or precedent. It is an
Ivy League institution with respect to the quality and dispositions of its
clientele and the fact that it has been, throughout most of its history, a
highly endowed and prestigeful private university. It departs from the
Ivy League pattern in its emphasis on its professional schools, mining,

engineering, medicine, law, and education, in its coeducational features, in its relatively brief history, and in its geographic removal from other major private universities. Its performance in the humanities shows a particular strength in the field of history both with respect to its baccalaureates who continue there or elsewhere and with respect to doctorates granted. Second to the history department, by a small margin, is the English department. Arts and philosophy are less than noteworthy. We should observe in passing, of course, that the history department at Stanford has benefited especially by its library acquisitions, in particular the Hoover Library on War, Revolution, and Peace, which is unique. But in the main, I am inclined to ascribe the undergraduate record of Stanford more to the quality of its students and their intellectual talents and dispositions than to any calculated policy of the institution designed to develop and magnify the humanities. Exception to this can probably be made only in the most recent decade. Stanford's record in the humanities, therefore, appears to have evolved despite, and not because of, administrative policy.

THREE MIDWESTERN STATE UNIVERSITIES

This chapter contains reports on three midwestern state universities of prime importance, the University of Wisconsin, Indiana University, and Ohio State University. Considerations governing their selection have been reviewed earlier. Their importance to this study lies in the contrast they provide to the Ivy League universities of the eastern seaboard, representing, as they do, a second great style of higher education on the current American scene.

Wisconsin

Of the three state universities considered in this chapter, the University of Wisconsin is the most venerable, and in the humanities by far the most distinguished. Wisconsin combines a land grant institution with a state university under a single roof, unlike Ohio State, which is exclusively a land grant institution, or Indiana, which has no land grant connections at all. Again, Wisconsin is among the first, if not the first, state university of the Midwest to attain a reputation as a center of scholarship and graduate study. According to Bernard Berelson,[1] Wisconsin by 1920 was one of the three state universities granting one per cent or more of the total doctorates in the United States; California (Berkeley) and Illinois were the other two. All during the 1930's, Wisconsin remained the only state university listed among the top five institutions most productive of doctorates. Ohio State emerges only later, and then with very strong concentration in sciences and technology; Indiana, according to Berelson, is not to be reckoned among larger graduate schools until the past decade, although its present acceleration is impressive.

Comparison between Wisconsin and California (Berkeley) is useful, since both are in the vanguard of state institutions that have risen to scholarly eminence. Like Berkeley, Wisconsin is the summit of a state system including community and junior colleges. Further, both institu-

[1] Bernard Berelson, *Graduate Education in the United States* (McGraw, 1960).

tions preserve a certain degree of independence from direct state control: more than half the revenues come from sources independent of legislative control, and a separate Board of Regents serves as cushion between the institution and the legislature. Finally, of course, Wisconsin and Berkeley have had a long-established and respected tradition of humanistic scholarship.

But there are important points of difference between the two schools. Wisconsin has not approached that degree of student selectivity that Berkeley maintains. Wisconsin has neither the population base nor the wealth to support the variety and structure represented by the California system of universities, colleges, and junior colleges. For many reasons, it becomes clear that Wisconsin is more oriented to utility and to service than is Berkeley. Agriculture, engineering, and teacher training are conspicuous features at Wisconsin; its researches, in such subjects as chemistry, dairying, and engineering, constitute a prime focus of the institution's energies, and are supported by abundant research grants, both federal and private. This practical bent has not been without its rewards; research led in one instance to the patenting of an insecticide, bringing substantial revenues to the institution. Differences are also to be observed in the constituency of the two institutions. The ethnic, cultural, and occupational backgrounds of the Wisconsin student differ in many respects from those at Berkeley. Primarily an agricultural state, Wisconsin's total population in 1960 was about three and a half million. California's population is approximately eleven million, with greater urbanization and per capita wealth. Despite these divergences, of the midwestern institutions considered, Wisconsin is more similar to Berkeley in point of history and characteristics than it is to Ohio State or Indiana.

The history of the humanities at Wisconsin possesses a certain dignity and, for this region, antiquity not shared by most midwestern institutions. By the turn of the century Wisconsin's department of history had achieved luminous distinction through the works of Frederick Jackson Turner and the economist John Rogers Commons. Shortly after this the regime of President Van Hise brought about a fortunate collaboration with the liberal and intellectual Senator LaFollette. This period saw the emergence of Wisconsin from provincialism to a university of rank by the early 1920's. Spanish and English literature were put on a very creditable basis and the German literature department had an international reputation. It was Van Hise who emphasized and extended the "Wisconsin Idea" of public service, which even today dominates the practical philosophy of the university.

Surveying the presidency of this institution over the past sixty years, it is interesting to note that only two of the presidents have taught in the humanities. Except for Presidents Dykstra (1937-45) and Harrington (1962-   ), all have taught in the natural sciences. This fact, characteristic of many midwestern universities, sharply contrasts with the presidential pattern in Ivy League institutions. The high degree of prestige accorded the humanities at Wisconsin becomes even more notable when one considers that it flourished under scientifically oriented presidents.

We observed in Chapter 3 that Wisconsin represents a fairly pure type of land grant institution, in terms of its pattern of contribution to different fields of scholarship. In fact, it proved to be one of the most typical of all in terms of its pattern of scholarly production. The characteristic of this emerging class, an emphasis upon industrial and particularly agricultural and biological sciences, does indeed characterize Wisconsin, and is entirely congruent with an abiding sense of service to the industries of the state that has been a shaping force for many decades.

The undergraduate record in the humanities at Wisconsin, obtained from the National Academy of Sciences, is given in Table 70.

TABLE 70. Baccalaureate graduates of Wisconsin who continued to a Ph.D. in humanities.

B.A. Year		Foreign Languages	History	English	Fine Arts and Music	Philosophy	Total
Before	M	4	2	4	—	1	11
1926	F	6	2	3	—	—	11
1926-35	M	15	17	17	8	5	62
	F	5	3	7	1	—	16
1936-45	M	6	25	17	15	3	66
	F	—	3	3	1	—	7
1946-59	M	12	24	19	2	10	67
	F	3	1	1	—	—	5

In point of over-all quantity, the numbers in the humanities are not as high as in the case of Berkeley, but the pattern is not greatly dissimilar. In both instances the history department possesses considerable vigor as compared with departments of English, foreign languages and literature. Arts and music are relatively strong at Wisconsin, probably because of the peculiar emphasis given music at this institution. Philosophy is not impressively strong at either. There appears to be a consistent and general tendency, in the western regions of this country, for the humanities to find their strongest support in history and weakest support in philosophy and the fine arts. This is sustained in the record at Wisconsin.

Both Berkeley and Wisconsin show a significant yield of humanistic scholars from among their undergraduates throughout all four periods under consideration, though the record of Berkeley shows evidence of its greater growth. The index, or rate per thousand B.A.'s, of humanistic scholarly production at Berkeley is approximately 50 per cent greater than at Wisconsin, and is, without question, a reflection of the latter's lower selectivity and greater commitment to service and utility. The science-humanities ratio, however, based on undergraduate origins of humanistic scholars, is 4.6, virtually identical with that of Berkeley.

Turning to Wisconsin's record in the granting of doctorates, Table 71 shows the number of doctorates granted by Wisconsin in the major areas of the curriculum, between 1936 and 1956. The vast majority are clearly in the physical and biological sciences, mainly the latter. Only about 1,100 degrees were granted in the social sciences and humanities, approximately equally divided. By contrast, the physical and biological sciences account for two and a half times that number. It is particularly interesting to compare this distribution with that of Berkeley.

TABLE 71. Ph.D. degrees granted by Wisconsin.

Ph.D. Year	Physical Sciences	Biological Sciences	Social Sciences	Humanities	Education	Other
1936-42	262	345	123	205	50	43
1943-49	266	397	98	83	66	35
1950-56	644	893	330	303	152	114
TOTAL	1,172	1,635	551	591	268	192

Berkeley's doctoral figures are remarkably similar to Wisconsin's, except in the second category, where the numbers in the biological sciences are 80 per cent greater at Wisconsin. This detail further confirms some of the differences that we educed between the character of these two institutions and the relatively greater "land grant" commitment of

Wisconsin. The Wisconsin science-humanities ratio among doctorates granted in this period is 4.7. This figure is far higher than that of any Ivy League or large private university, but it is notably lower than most land grant institutions other than Berkeley.

The record of recent doctorates granted in the humanities at Wisconsin is contained in Table 72. It reveals few surprises. The arts are notably weak, history and English conspicuously strong. Philosophy, though it is obviously rising, produces comparatively few doctorates. The picture here is altogether congruent with that of undergraduates continuing to the doctorate (see Table 70).

TABLE 72. Ph.D. degrees in humanities granted
by Wisconsin.

Ph.D. Year	Foreign Languages	History	English	Fine Arts and Music	Philosophy	Total
1936-42	83	52	60	4	6	205
1943-49	23	30	26	1	3	83
1950-56	54	123	113	4	9	303
TOTAL	160	205	199	9	18	591

Wisconsin draws its graduate students in humanities from diverse geographic regions: 33 per cent are from eastern schools and New England; 5 per cent are from the Pacific Coast. Thus, geographically speaking, Wisconsin is surprisingly cosmopolitan. Again, with respect to the type of institution from which it draws (especially considering its geographic region), Wisconsin presents a very wide spectrum. Slightly less than half its graduate students in humanities come from public institutions and of the remainder, 30 per cent come from nonsectarian, private institutions, while 21 per cent come from church-supported Protestant, Jewish, and Catholic institutions. Only 18 per cent took their undergraduate degrees at the university itself. Particularly interesting is a comparison of these figures with those for the Ivy League schools investigated, namely, Harvard and Yale. By comparison, these two Ivy League schools turn out to be rather strikingly "provincial."

Something should be said about female baccalaureates who continue to the doctorate in this institution. They are few but not insignificant in number; as may be seen in Table 70, there have been only 12 since the baccalaureate class of 1936. These figures are difficult to interpret in view of the long time lapse between B.A. and Ph.D., especially for female scholars in the humanities. The record, however, is remarkably similar to that at Berkeley and suggests that this type of institution is not claiming an increasing proportion of female scholars in the humanities in more recent years.

Finally, it is useful to ask how much lapsed time exists between baccalaureate and doctorate at Wisconsin. The figures show that Wisconsin provides the fastest and most efficient pathway to the Ph.D. of any public university in the nation, with an average time of 9.3 years for men. The figure of women, who are comparatively few in number, is somewhat longer, namely 13.3 years.

Since World War II, a number of curricular and administrative changes have occurred at Wisconsin that have influenced the position of the humanities. The first of these is the establishment in 1946 of a two-year integrated Liberal Studies Program that has annually claimed a substantial portion of the freshman class. It is limited to 300 students annually. This type of "honors" program is not without its parallel in better state universities, but its early inception at Wisconsin probably indicates the respected position of the humanities there. In 1957 the Institute for the Advancement of the Humanities, under the leadership of Marshall Claggett, classics scholar and medieval historian, was established. In a university dominated throughout most of its history by chemical and biological research, this represents a rather special development. The Institute remains a modest enterprise, but it represents the unprecedented departure of maintaining several humanistic scholars who are full-time researchers, not teachers.

Wisconsin's attainments in the area of fine arts and music, especially in recruiting undergraduates (who will go on to their doctorates probably elsewhere) are probably due to its well-known School of Music, founded in the late nineteenth century. Originally concerned with preparing secondary-school teachers, Wisconsin, since around 1930, has won a reputation for scholarly consideration of music. Possibly, the special emphasis given music at Wisconsin lies in the cultural influence of the very large music-loving German constituency that earlier made Wisconsin a center of German scholarship.

I shall forego any attempt at special interpretation of the records of Wisconsin's other departments. It is clear that in recent years, in the granting of Ph.D.'s at least, the history, English, and foreign language departments have borne the main burden, while philosophy and fine arts have been notably thin. The most impressive department is probably history, followed closely thereafter by English, which can boast of having on its faculty one of the most famous female English scholars in America.

It is necessary to make some kind of summary estimate of the position of the humanities in this university and to indicate the forces that have made possible their emergence in a climate in many respects seemingly inhospitable. We have had occasion to compare California (Berkeley) with Wisconsin and it is clear that they are both in the very forefront of state universities in the development of significant graduate programs. If anything, Wisconsin, for reasons that we shall presently surmise, arrived earlier than Berkeley or any other midwestern institution to the status of a major graduate university and a major contributor to the humanities. In the past 40 years the race has been to Berkeley. It has been larger, more exclusive, more endowed, and, in many other respects has claimed advantages. But, as we have noted, the statistical parallel between the two institutions is striking.

One question remains unanswered: why did the humanities, and higher scholarship in general, find their home so early and so surely at Wisconsin rather than at other state institutions in the Midwest? At the present time one might name Michigan, Minnesota, and Illinois as almost equally strong in the humanities, but the records cited by Berelson and others show that this claim could not have been made thirty years ago. I do not presume to know the final answer, but it would appear plausible that there was something of fortune and something of character in the intellectual fate of this Northern Lake State. As one observer put it, "Scholarship in the humanities found its haven here early as a result of particular men, and a fortunate political and intellectual climate." Thus for at least six decades there has been a humanistic and scholarly tradition at Wisconsin, founded in history, literature, and languages, that has been proved resistant to displacement and has never lost out to vocationalism, technology, and other claims upon the university's resources.

Indiana

The story of Indiana University is easier to tell than that of any institution considered heretofore, and the reason is plain: as a scholarly institution it has little anchorage to the past. Berelson points out that until 1950, Indiana was not to be included among the universities granting one per cent or more of the doctorates granted in all American institutions.[2] Of the twenty-nine major universities included in this class at that time, Indiana tied with UCLA for twenty-eighth place. In the decade from 1925 to 1935, for example, Indiana granted approximately sixteen doctorates per year, of which only two were in the humanities. Why Indiana, established in 1822, lagged so far behind such institutions as Minnesota, Michigan, Wisconsin, and Illinois is not entirely clear. A number of factors probably conspired to this end. One major reason that emerges was its lack of any conspicuous educational leadership at any point in its early history. Moreover, its admissions standards were consistently low, and the financial support tenuous. Purdue, the great land grant rival of Indiana, appeared to command greater public respect and endorsement in this region of the country because of its strong emphasis on practical, utilitarian aspects of education. Indiana's weakness in the humanities was evidently not offset by any great strength in the technologies.

Over a span of thirty-five years, from 1902 to 1937, the presidency was held by William L. Bryan, a Greek scholar by training, but a man who allegedly retained the office long after he had become out of step with the times. Older members of the present Indiana faculty describe the prevailing atmosphere of the university during the 1920's and 1930's as "leisurely," "indulgent," and "paternalistic," and, as we shall presently see, there was little to indicate any real intellectual vitality or direction in the institution.

The history of Indiana in the past quarter of a century is intimately bound up with a particular figure, President Herman B. Wells, who assumed the presidency in 1937. Born in Indiana and a graduate of its state university, it has been said of Wells that every third citizen in the state was his uncle, cousin, nephew, or niece. It is noteworthy that all presidents of Indiana from 1893 until the present have been native sons and graduates of the university itself. This tendency to select native sons as presidents of midwestern state universities is possibly related partly to regional loyalty and partly to the inevitable affiliation of the state university with state political control. No comparable relationship exists for Ivy League institutions. It would appear that the university found in Wells a most extraordinary president, whose qualifications

2 *Ibid.*, p. 93.

at the outset were by no means impressive. He had never earned a doctorate degree and the interests of his early years were in business and financial management. After some fifteen years of varied experience outside of academic circles, he eventually became a dean and a professor in the School of Business Administration in the mid-1930's. Few educators in America would have reposed great hopes in a man whose acquaintance with the academic world was so slender and whose scholarly attainments were so small.

President Wells, furthermore, arrived on the scene at an awkward moment in the history of American education, at the end of the depression and just before the onset of World War II, which was to paralyze educational development for almost a decade. Consequently, it was not until after the war that Wells became an effective force. In the past two decades, however, Indiana has witnessed astounding developments in the humanities and in other areas as well, which have brought it to the forefront of midwestern universities. This transformation has been due in part to the demands of the times, in part to an affluent postwar society, but in the main, I believe, to the educational statemanship exercised by President Wells.

Much of what President Wells has accomplished at Indiana does not appear in this book's statistics. Indiana was, in fact, initially selected because of its relatively obscure and undistinguished performance in the humanities as well as in other divisions. It is clear that within the past decade and at an accelerating rate, the university is becoming a vital and buoyant intellectual center, especially in the humanistic area. It is less profitable here than in other cases to review the statistical record. I shall do so, however, in the need to point out certain facts. But the reader should be forewarned that the full truth of the present status of Indiana can be understood only in terms of comments to be made hereafter and is not manifest from the statistics.[3]

In Chapter 2, it will be recalled, a factor analysis was undertaken, based upon the undergraduate record of the ninety-five most productive institutions in the nation for the period 1936-56. It might have been expected that Indiana would fall among the second category of

---

[3] A recent publication of the National Academy of Sciences, *Doctoral Production of United States Universities, 1920-62,* Publication 1142, includes more recent data on this point. The expectation that Indiana University should show a sharp rise in the most recent period is well confirmed by this document, but the figures for humanistic production are classified in such a manner that it is not possible to separate them from those granted in other fields.

institutions, that in which most state universities and land grant institutions were clustered. In fact, Indiana turns out to be something of a maverick, showing no high identification with any of the four clusters. It departs from the pattern of most public institutions in being relatively weak in the biological and physical sciences, and the technologies, a not surprising fact, considering that neighboring Purdue has achieved such great technological distinction.

Table 73 shows the number of baccalaureates in the university who continued to the doctoral level in different fields of the humanities. The numbers are surely not impressive compared with most of the institutions that have been reviewed. Since World War II only twenty-four baccalaureates at Indiana have taken a doctorate in the humanities; on the basis of our interpolation, the record stands at about three per year. The average for the years before the war is about the same.

TABLE 73. Baccalaureate graduates of Indiana who continued to a Ph.D. in humanities.

B.A. Year		Foreign Languages	History	English	Fine Arts and Music	Philosophy	Total
Before	M	—	4	2	—	—	6
1926	F	5	—	3	—	—	8
1926-35	M	8	2	7	2	—	19
	F	3	1	—	—	—	4
1936-45	M	6	10	7	1	—	24
	F	2	4	1	—	—	7
1946-59	M	6	9	9	4	3	31
	F	—	2	—	2	—	4

History stands numerically first; languages and English follow closely. This record does not show the recent upsurge in baccalaureate graduates going on to their Ph.D. since 1956. The post-1956 change is greater here than at any other institution analyzed in this book.

The production of doctorates, shown in Table 74, strikingly shows the comparatively low number of degrees in physical and biological sciences, and the extremely high number of doctorates in education. The science-humanities ratio for doctorates granted, which I have regarded as a particularly revealing figure, stands, in the case of Indiana, at 2.25, one of the lowest obtained by any state institution. This is a direct reflection of the degree to which the sciences and technologies are excluded from the state university and concentrated on at Purdue.

TABLE 74. Ph.D. degrees granted by Indiana.

Ph.D. Year	Physical Sciences	Biological Sciences	Social Sciences	Humanities	Education	Other
1936-42	79	18	17	25	31	—
1943-49	61	25	27	18	58	2
1950-56	142	87	158	140	422	59
TOTAL	282	130	202	183	511	61

The Indiana ratio is far below Wisconsin's 4.7, and not too far away from Harvard's 1.2 or Yale's 1.4. Indiana's pattern would thus bear some resemblance to that of an Ivy League institution were it not for Indiana's overwhelming concentration in education.

The record of doctorates granted in the humanities in recent times is contained in Table 75. As might be expected from the record of un-

TABLE 75. Ph.D. degrees in humanities granted by Indiana.

Ph.D. Year	Foreign Languages	History	English	Fine Arts and Music	Philosophy	Total
1936-42	3	17	5	—	—	25
1943-49	1	8	9	—	—	18
1950-56	13	43	35	44	5	140
TOTAL	17	68	49	44	5	183

dergraduates in humanistic scholarship, history and English are particularly vigorous, whereas languages are notably low. The record of forty-four doctorates granted in the arts since 1956 reflects an extraordinary growth in music scholarship at Indiana. Most Ph.D.'s are in the field of music theory and musicology, although some are in musical education. Philosophy has been unproductive, but activity in this field has increased since 1956.

Let us now consider the recruitment pattern that characterizes humanistic scholars at Indiana. Over half of the humanities graduate students at Indiana come from the eastern Midwest (although only 18 per cent are Indiana baccalaureates), with another 20 per cent attracted from New England and the North Atlantic states. This high degree of student recruitment from its own part of the country tends to confirm the regionalism that I concluded in Chapter 7 to be typical of students enrolled in humanities graduate departments of all major universities. Even Wisconsin, which is the most cosmopolitan of midwestern schools in recruitment of humanist scholars, takes in 50 per cent of them from its own part of the country. (See Table 4.)

Finally, a comment should be made concerning the interval between B.A. and Ph.D. at Indiana in the humanities. It is comparatively brief, standing at 9.9 years for men and 13.0 years for women. Only Wisconsin, among state universities, has a shorter time-lapse for men.

As pointed out earlier, the most unusual developments of Indiana have occurred in the past decade, particularly as they affect the humanities. During this period virtually every department in the humanities has been expanded, both in staff and physical facilities. A major structure now houses the departments of languages, literature, and history; a center for linguistic studies has been established; and at the present time a new and major art center is being completed. Before the construction of this art center, the fine arts were housed in quarters that lacked proper galleries. Again, only in the last half decade has the new theater and concert hall been completed, a commodious and impressive structure. A center of philosophic and logical research is also being established. In many of the recent appointments in the humanities, scholars have been attracted to Indiana from the East and from Europe, lending these departments a cosmopolitanism they clearly lacked before.

The prevailing spirit at this institution today, while elusive in some respects, is on the whole quite evident, and gives Indiana a definitive style and quality. The university obviously has advanced from relative obscurity into the forefront of midwestern universities, with particular recent benefit to the humanities. The sense of optimism and well-being that prevails is immediately impressive. There seems to be remarkably little complaint and friction, while at the same time there is a keen anticipation of future growth and progress.

One is particularly struck at Indiana with the nice balance between the ideals of public service and the support of scholarship that, from the public point of view, would undoubtedly be described as "esoteric." The recently constructed Union Building constitutes a very special kind of university center. Its facilities are made available to all manner of public service organizations, whether identified with the university or not. Its role as a community center has succeeded pre-eminently in establishing a close bond between this university and the surrounding constituency.

Before concluding, it might be interesting to record here the reaction of a high official at Indiana to the four indictments of the state university made by the Ivy League dean whom I earlier quoted. To the first charge, that the state university is subject to direct and uninformed political control, he replied that he knew of no such instance, pointing to the fact that the Kinsey research was accomplished at the university without the slightest protest from either the public or their legislative representatives. On the other hand, he continued, private institutions in some cases have had clerical sponsors to contend with, and in others, very powerful alumni pressures. To the second criticism, the charge of indiscriminate admissions policy, his first response was that the state university is becoming more discriminating than it was; on the other hand, he pointed out, criteria and methods of selection were so imperfect that it would be hazardous to attempt the refined judgments made by exclusive private institutions. The third criticism of the state university was that it is inevitably pressured into vocationalism and utilitarianism in its educational program. His reply to this assertion was that, at least in the case of Indiana, one must understand that the American university is an institutional invention and that in its character it combines the pure liberal arts tradition with a variety of other functions not traditionally associated with the European, or for that matter the Ivy League, institution. Finally, to the charge that state universities are too large and impersonal, he pointed out that in the end this is equally true of the public high schools as they are evolving and of adult society itself, so that the large university is in many respects a better preparation for life than the small, intimate liberal arts college with its spurious protectiveness and intimacy. On the other hand, he insisted that the university was far less impersonal than it might seem because it consists of a large number of fairly small intimate communities revolving around departments, fraternities, and dormitories; the faculty, in fact, have often taken upon themselves the role of dormitory counselors, promoting considerable student-faculty contact on the personal level.

A summary in the case of Indiana can be very brief since, historically speaking, its attainment in the production of humanistic scholars is unimpressive. Perhaps the most important thing to remember is that the unusual vigor of humanistic scholarship at the present moment has been brought about by the educational statesmanship of the president and other administrative officers, and stimulated by the fact that the humanities within the state system devolve in a special sense upon the university and not its rival, Purdue, which assumes major responsibility in the areas of science and the technologies. This division of labor is auspicious for the development of the humanities at Indiana.

Ohio State

The third public institution of the Midwest that I visited was Ohio State. Its large size, its almost unconditional commitment to public service, its land grant status, and its weakness in the humanities as compared with professional, technological, and scientific areas prompted me to select it for study. By all odds it is the most important state institution in Ohio, quite overshadowing Ohio and Miami Universities within the state system, and is one of the ten largest state institutions in the nation. Apart from its main campus in Columbus, it has five outlying extension centers scattered about the state. The main body of the institution, including practically all of the professional schools, is located at Columbus. These professional schools include colleges of dentistry, law, medicine, nursing, optometry, pharmacy, and veterinary medicine. In the undergraduate program there are now approximately 17,000 students, of whom all but a small fraction are at the Columbus campus. Of these undergraduates, approximately 5,000 took majors within the College of Arts and Sciences.

This institution is a radical departure from Ivy League schools, and in a number of respects is different from the state institutions reviewed heretofore. Of particular importance is the concentration of graduate students in vocational and professional training, and the relatively small proportion in arts and sciences. One might describe this as an arts and sciences college immersed in a much larger community whose primary educational purposes are directed toward practical aims, the focus and the intent that inspired the establishment of land grant institutions in the beginning.

The position of Ohio State in the educational pattern of Ohio deserves some comment. Ohio University proper, located in the southern part of the state, has never commanded the popular support that Ohio State has claimed, nor has it benefited from the land grant subsidies of the latter. Its enrollment has been relatively small; it has drawn its student body from a relatively impoverished, agrarian section of the state; and its attainments in the realm of higher scholarship are far exceeded by Ohio State. Thus, in this state, the balance between land grant and the state universities, which were here kept separate, has been heavily in favor of the land grant institution. Beyond this, it should be noted that the state of Ohio is unusually well endowed with liberal arts colleges of excellent reputation and that there is also a very important private university, Western Reserve, in Cleveland. Thus, the competition that Ohio State faces in its efforts to attract students of humanistic leanings is not so much from the state university as from an unusual number of small, quality colleges. It is reasonable to surmise that students interested in the humanities would find their natural attraction to these institutions, whereas those intent upon vocational and technological training would be drawn to Ohio State.

One thing is certain: Ohio State expressly conceives its function to be one of service to all citizens of the state. Looking at the total enrollment reported at Ohio State in the Annual Report for 1959-60, one finds that of a total of 29,000 students, over 26,000 come from Ohio itself. Of the remainder, 500 are foreign students, while the rest are thinly distributed from the surrounding regions, with approximately 700 from New York and Pennsylvania. Furthermore, in the Annual Report of the Registrar and Examiner for 1959-60, one finds the following statement: "Ohio State University is state supported. As such it feels a primary responsibility to the residents of Ohio. We admit into the University all graduates of 12th grade high schools in the State of Ohio." The resultant relative laxity in admission standards that prevails to the present time is one of the conspicuous characteristics of this institution. In some of the colleges within the university, more students come from the lower third than the upper third of their high school class. Even in the arts and sciences approximately one out of seven of the freshmen comes from that lower third. There is an almost black-and-white contrast between the intense selectivity of many private institutions, especially in the East, and this "land grant democracy," supporting the feelings of our Ivy League dean about selectivity in state universities. In summary, it seems fair to say that of the public institutions considered in our study, Ohio State is the least selective, while California (Berkeley) is the most selective.

The history of Ohio State offers little ground for speculation or excitement. The university has grown steadily, particularly since the turn of the century. In 1900 it had 1,200 students, by 1920, 8,000, by 1930, almost 15,000; it shows a falling off as the G.I. Bill expired and then a steady rise to new heights at the present time. It is clear that Ohio

State has never attracted great leaders to its presidency. For one thing, it has appeared to be a rule that the office is reserved for native sons of the state; at least, all presidents from the turn of the century to the present have been such.

Some indication of the growth and development of Ohio State may be judged by the period in which it first made important contributions to graduate scholarship. This turning point has been called by Berelson "genuine entry to graduate study" and defined by him as the point at which a university grants one per cent or more of the doctorates awarded annually in the United States. Ohio State emerged to this position by 1925, along with some half dozen other state institutions, making it not among the first ten, but among the first twenty in the development of graduate programs.

Given the character of the institution one would not expect the record of Ohio State in the production of humanistic scholars to be high, despite the fact that it has an extraordinarily large student body. The relatively low selection standards and the very heavy commitment to vocational and professional training in education, business, technology, and sciences would support such expectations. Statistics confirmed them. In Chapter 2 it was found that Ohio State identified primarily with land grant, and secondarily with technological, classes of institutions. This reflects its commitment to the biological and physical sciences and technology, and its relative weakness in the humanities.

The record of undergraduates who have continued to the doctorate in the humanities is again not impressive when compared with eastern private institutions, or, for that matter, with Berkeley or Wisconsin. Still the absolute numbers are respectable, as shown in Table 76. The distribution of scholars across the several fields leaves little occasion for comment save to observe that philosophy appears to have been historically weak at this institution, while the history department, as in most midwestern institutions, holds a slight margin of advantage. It may also be observed that there are small but continuing numbers of women graduates who continue to the doctorate level, especially in the field of languages.

The male index of humanistic production for Periods III and IV stands at about three doctorates per thousand baccalaureates, roughly one-third the rate at Wisconsin and half that at Indiana. Probably, however, no great importance should be attached to these differences, in view of the degree to which Ohio State includes substantial

TABLE 76. Baccalaureates of Ohio State who continued to a Ph.D. in humanities.

B.A. Year		Foreign Languages	History	English	Fine Arts and Music	Philosophy	Total
Before	M	1	2	6	—	—	9
1926	F	4	1	1	—	—	6
1926-35	M	11	3	6	5	—	25
	F	4	1	4	1	—	10
1936-45	M	5	13	7	5	1	31
	F	3	—	2	2	—	7
1946-59	M	11	11	6	1	1	30
	F	2	—	—	1	—	3

percentages in vocational and applied programs that preclude serious exposure to the humanities. But in terms of the historical records, it is clear that the Ohio State graduate who continues to a doctorate in the humanities is an exceedingly rare person.

Finally, as a confirmation of the foregoing conclusions, I calculated the ratio of those baccalaureates who have continued to their doctorate in the sciences to those who have continued in the humanities, as earlier reported. It stands at 6.3, one of the highest ratios obtaining among publicly supported institutions that cannot be classified outright as technological schools.

The record of doctorate degrees granted is shown in Table 77 for the major areas of the curriculum between 1936 and 1956; one observes that the number of doctorates granted in the sciences is many times greater than that in the humanities.

TABLE 77. Ph.D. degrees granted by Ohio State.

Ph.D. Year	Physical Sciences	Biological Sciences	Social Sciences	Humanities	Education
1936-42	262	150	117	75	115
1943-49	250	150	133	66	128
1950-56	544	402	339	120	240
TOTAL	1,056	702	589	261	483

This ratio stands at 6.7, or slightly greater than the ratio among undergraduates continuing to the doctorate in these areas. Doctorates in education total almost twice those granted in the humanistic disciplines. Here again, the vocational and utilitarian quality of the institution is further confirmed.

Table 78 presents the numbers of doctorates granted in recent decades in the various humanistic fields. The English department seems consistently the strongest, while of recent date the number of degrees granted in the arts is above expectation. In the main, the record is well balanced among the several humanistic disciplines.

TABLE 78. Ph.D. degrees in humanities granted by
Ohio State.

Ph.D. Year	Foreign Languages	History	English	Fine Arts and Music	Philosophy	Total
1936-42	23	22	23	1	6	75
1943-49	18	19	24	—	5	66
1950-56	25	23	39	29	4	120
TOTAL	66	64	86	30	15	261

The figures for the arts are somewhat difficult to interpret, however, since these degrees may be awarded in part for performance and in part for art education, as well as for scholarly research in the history of art, so heavily emphasized in eastern private universities.

I have had occasion earlier to note that undergraduates at Ohio State tend to be very heavily recruited from the state of Ohio itself. The doctoral candidates in the humanities show a considerably greater degree of geographical dispersion, with slightly better than 50 per cent of them coming from the eastern Midwest, while the northeast section of the country contributes almost a quarter, and the Pacific Coast 7 per cent. Once again the humanistic graduate students are about equally divided between those coming from public and private institutions, while only 18 per cent are Ohio State baccalaureates. Thus, at the graduate level in humanities the picture of the student body is one of relative cosmopolitanism as compared with an undergraduate picture of very heavy concentrations in the state itself. In part, this may be due to the necessity of having a very large staff of graduate assistants to serve in the language, English, and history courses provided for the general student body, rather than to any calculated policy of drawing students from varied regions and institutions. Further, the low recruitment of graduate assistants among Ohio State's own baccalaureates probably reflects the relatively small number attracted to humanistic vocations.

One final note on the character of the graduate program in the humanities should be made on the lapsed time between B.A. and Ph.D., which tends to be relatively long, standing at 11.3 years for men and 13.3 years for women. This is the highest of any institution reported here in detail, and is consistent with the impression that most humanistic doctorates at Ohio State are granted to candidates who have served protracted periods as half-time teaching assistants.

Are there any forces in movement, such as we have observed in Indiana, to redress what many educators would consider an imbalance between the humanities and vocational training at this institution? Any positive answer to this question must be heavily qualified. It is true that the construction of the new fine arts center is underway, and that a music building was constructed slightly over a decade ago. Still, both of these seem more directed toward the cultivation of performance and composition in the arts than toward scholarly research of the sort leading to the doctorate in eastern institutions. The departments of languages, English, and history, it appears, are still primarily devoted to the service of the larger student body and characteristically show massive enrollments at the undergraduate level and particularly in first and second year courses. They remain as ancillary services to the great majority of undergraduates intent upon vocational and professional pursuits. The humanities departments at Ohio State appear less emancipated for scholarly enterprise and more bound to pedagogical routine than those of any institution reviewed in this study. Comparable conditions probably existed in the humanities at Indiana a decade or two ago. The difference lies in the special liberation and support of humanistic scholarship at Indiana in recent times.

In summary, I have been dealing here with a relatively pure and justly famous example of the land grant institution, with all that this implies about the pursuit of such goals as utility, service, and educational democracy. Characteristically, students are unselected, locally recruited, and disposed to the useful and the practical in educational aims. Among them the humanities are rarely selected as a serious scholarly career. The humanities departments find themselves laboring under very heavy pedagogical burdens while their scholarly pursuits are not provided with strong institutional support. It is plain here that the humanities cry for greater support and a more dignified role within the curriculum and life of the community.

ASSESSMENT AND SUMMARY

It has been my special privilege in the course of this study to interview perhaps two hundred persons of whom the greater part were humanistic scholars. I did not address them with a set schedule of questions for reasons I have already made clear. Persons who are interested in a tabulation of the opinions of humanists on educational matters as compared with scholars in other fields will find in Bernard Berelson's *Graduate Education in the United States,* which is a most useful and informative compendium, an excellent summary of data of this kind. He demonstrates in clear statistical terms that humanistic scholars differ from scientists with respect to their attitudes toward teaching, their pattern of scholarly production, and their style of publication, among other things. He also shows, in data supplied to me, the special tendency of humanistic scholars to engage in solitary rather than corporate researches. Thus, while it is common in the sciences for publications to be issued under multiple authorship, this is a rare practice in the humanities.

While I have not compiled the same type of statistical data that Berelson reports, I have nevertheless developed a body of impressions concerning the condition of the several humanistic disciplines and the outlooks of humanistic scholars that bear recording. Let me begin by discussing the five humanistic areas under consideration in this study.

History

Of all the disciplines reviewed in this study it seems to me that history is in the most fortunate circumstances. Its recruitment is the most diverse both geographically and with respect to the type of institution from which it draws its membership. Then, too, it is numerically the largest, exceeding the field of English by a very small margin. Moreover, it is my clear impression that historians have a surer confidence both in their mission and their effectiveness than scholars in other humanistic disciplines. They are not torn by any major schism, they less often complain of their isolation from the mainstream of the intellectual life of their times, and they are by all odds the most directly and intimately involved with the affairs of their age.

In fact, the discipline of history has for a century or more produced men who have had intimate part in the shaping of public, political, and governmental action. Some, such as McMahon, have served in public office and others, such as Turner, have drafted an intellectual outlook that found powerful expression in the management of public affairs. In the present time, we have notable examples of members of the historical fraternity serving in positions of high office in the government, in diplomatic service, and in important advisory positions. It was no extraordinary thing that the Secretary of State delivered an address to the American Historical Association only two years ago.

It is interesting to contrast the American Historical Association and its membership with the typical professional association for scientists. Whereas scientific associations usually require a doctorate for membership, recognize multiple divisions, provide standards for certification in varying degrees, and otherwise are encumbered with complicated bureaucratic trappings, the American Historical Association is remarkably direct and simple in its conception. There is no specification that one must hold a doctoral degree for membership, nor that a person occupy an academic post. The requirement is simply that the individual have concern with history as a sphere of scholarship. Included in the membership of this association, beyond the academics, are newspaper editors, persons in government service, novelists, and others. In short, the fraternity of historians encompasses substantial numbers who lie quite beyond the pale of an academic environment. This probably brings a freshness and vitality to its ranks that is absent in many scientific associations.

Another quality of the historian that impressed me was the absence of any rigorous commitment to methodology. In this regard the historians are remarkably free as compared, for example, with economists, sociologists, and other social scientists. The premium upon sagacity and style to which I alluded in my first chapter seems to apply here with special force. The discipline unquestionably attracts to its ranks individuals who are sensitive at once to literary values and factual reality.

I have sought in the foregoing to present a picture of the condition of historical scholarship as particularly attractive. But there are, all the same, some significant movements afoot that may alter this picture somewhat. For example, it appeared generally true that younger historians tended to think of themselves as primarily social scientists while older members of the fraternity identified with the humanities. It is probably a sound surmise that history will become increasingly identified with the social sciences and less allied with literature in the future. It is probably also important to note that American historiography is rapidly outgrowing its earlier provincialism. In former times most American historians were concerned with American history. In recent decades this situation has rapidly altered so that now European and Asiatic history constitute an ever increasing focus of scholarly attention.

The Arts

The distinctive thing about scholarship in the arts among our humanistic disciplines is its late arrival on the American scene. Numerically the arts remain the smallest of the fields under consideration. Only in the 1930's, and then largely in the Ivy League universities, was graduate scholarship in this field established. It remains in our time still geographically concentrated. Thus, for example, over 50 per cent of the doctorates granted in arts were given by institutions in New England and the Mid-Atlantic states. If we include the East North Central states, we can account for 75 per cent. One has the impression that this area of humanistic scholarship has much room for growth and that large segments of the American collegiate population are never properly exposed to the fine arts. In contrast with history, the arts remain geographically concentrated with respect to their scholarly centers and recruitment of adherents.

There is further within this field a conflict concerning the ideal of scholarship that should be fostered. The Ph.D. in fine arts as it was established in eastern Ivy League universities involved essentially historical research. It followed what one professor described as the Boethian doctrine that maintained that the true artist is not the composer or the performer, but rather the appreciator. In contrast, there is a growing tendency, largely in western state institutions, to grant a doctorate in this field recognizing artistic composition, and performances or even proficiency in teaching in lieu of the traditional dissertation. The real conflict is between those who emphasize historical research as opposed to those recognizing composition. The program at the State University of Iowa, for example, shows almost exclusively the western pattern. At Indiana the music department grants degrees for both historical scholarship and composition. At Berkeley the music department is initiating a doctorate in composition, while the fine arts department there offers no comparable degree.

This schism will unquestionably be brought to some resolution in the course of time. The doctorate in composition is likely to prevail in most western and public institutions, and, indeed, may invade the Ivy League institutions in time. It is probably also true that scholarship will extend itself to regions and institutions now relatively untouched. There remains, however, a rather serious obstacle, the fact that the great museum collections of the nation are sharply limited to the eastern seaboard and cannot be effectively transported. Thus, the fine arts may continue to retain a greater geographic concentration than other humanistic disciplines.

Philosophy

Philosophy, like the arts, tends to show a marked regional concentration. Approximately 55 per cent of the doctorates granted in this field are given by institutions in the New England and Mid-Atlantic states, while the Atlantic seaboard grants over 70 per cent. Moreover, as we have noted, Catholic institutions, and especially Catholic University of America, grant a very large number of doctorates in this field as compared with other areas. In fact, of doctorates granted in philosophy between 1936 and 1956, over a tenth come from Catholic University alone.

Just as the arts are divided by a schism, so is philosophy. This is in part a conflict of generations, but in part involves different conceptions of the scholarly task. Philosophers of the older school were inclined to address themselves to basic ethical and metaphysical questions, were direct in their concern with human problems, and strongly identified with the humanistic tradition. In the past several decades, however, there has grown up a group of philosophers who are primarily interested in modern logic and, broadly speaking, epistemology. Though initially guided by European examples, they have come to establish themselves in their native land with considerable vigor and with a strong sense of dedication. Without question they identify themselves less with the humanists than with linguists and mathematicians. In some institutions, as Indiana, the two schools of thought stand side by side, though maintaining some administrative separation. One proponent of the older philosophic tradition likened the fraternity of logicians to "carpenters who forever sharpen their tools and never cut a board." On the other hand, proponents of the modern logical inquiry insist that they are developing methods of unprecedented power for the direction of intellectual inquiry. It is clear to me, however, that the logicians, however astute and timely their contributions, are scarcely to be included in the humanistic fraternity by any reasonable criterion. They, themselves, commonly declare their allegiances with others.

English

Next to history, English is the largest of the humanistic disciplines in point of numbers. But English scholars do not, it appears to me, share the same sense of purpose and well-being that I ascribed to historians. In the first place, in most institutions the English faculty is called upon to provide a kind of service instruction in English grammar and literature survey courses that is frequently repetitious and unrewarding. Thus, for example, at one state university the English faculty numbers approximately 160, but their duties are very heavily taken up in providing basic instruction to the 20,000 undergraduates enrolled in all departments and professional schools. Certainly many English professors find the performance of such tasks a burdensome deflection from their true intellectual and scholarly interests.

That English literature is a clearly defined subject matter is beyond question. But one doubts that the teachers of English have a defined methodology or mode of approach. It would be more proper to say that they have plural methodology. Thus, in some instances English literature is approached from the point of view of rhetorical and syntactical structure; again, it may be viewed in terms of the psychological characteristics or autobiographical revelation of the author; or it may be examined in an effort to demonstrate how literature illuminates the sociology of an epoch. In short, there seems to be no consensus that defines the mode by which English literature shall be reviewed. In consequence, scholarship in this field invokes a kind of eclecticism of approach, frequently borrowing from other disciplines as it suits the scholars' purposes in the application of literature.

Another observation of this field is worth making, that is, the separation of scholarship and creative writing. While the historian does not separate the critical from the creative function, the English scholar does so to a rather striking degree. The separation between English bards and Scotch reviewers, which I have mentioned earlier, applies here with particular force. It is excessively rare to find a significant creative writer occupying a chair in a major university or holding a doctoral degree in English literature.

Just as the fine arts tend to be geographically limited in part through historical accident, but also in part because of the concentration of material resources, so English suffers to a lesser extent in the same fashion. The great libraries of the eastern seaboard are virtually without duplication west of the Appalachians, and they constitute a Mecca that attracts senior scholars in English literature. These in turn attract talented graduate students. This concentration can, however, be overstated; some of the major state universities, for instance, are rapidly developing distinguished library collections of their own.

Foreign Languages and Literature

If history is the most fortunate of the humanistic disciplines, it appears to me that foreign languages are the least fortunate, and this for several reasons. In the first place, scholars in this field find themselves called upon in the academic environment to devote the major part of their efforts to elementary or intermediate instruction in the language they profess. Thus, there is a heavy burden of dull and repetitious pedagogy for most of this group of scholars. Most professors of foreign language try to solace themselves with the thought that they are purveying not merely a language but a culture or civilization. They know, however, that they succeed in this enterprise with only an occasional few.

There is another source of discontent among professors of foreign languages. Usually they have a strong identification with the country whose language and civilization they teach. Yet they find themselves geographically alienated from their cultural homeland. It is thus a common thing for many of them at the first opportunity to betake themselves to the country of their cultural adoption. There are, however, some interesting developments in the foreign language field. The first of these is the recent significant government subsidy in the teaching of languages. Again, the development of various electronic and technical devices has greatly aided the acquisition of language skills. Finally, instruction in non-European languages such as Russian and Chinese, previously almost entirely neglected, has become widespread.

Much of what may be said concerning the character of scholarship in this area would merely repeat comments made concerning English scholarship, but perhaps one should make note here of the special area of linguistics. This kind of interdisciplinary excursion has shown rapid growth in a number of institutions and provides a fresh and stimulating scholarly departure for persons in foreign languages.

Such, it appears to me in quick summary, is the condition of the several humanistic fields examined in this study. It now seems appropriate to turn again to an examination of the basis for unity among these several fields. It might be profitable to examine certain propositions that persistently recurred in my conversations, most, if not all, of which are germane to this issue. I shall accordingly present nine of these propositions with a short discussion indicating the degree to which I consider them subject to greater or lesser qualification.

1. *That the humanities remain deeply committed to European intellectual traditions and not fully assimilated in the indigenous intellectual life of America.* It is probably true that the humanities, more than other disciplines, tend to look to European models. The fact that the humanities' "homeland" is the eastern seaboard is probably not without significance in this regard. But more important, their subject matter, especially in art, history, English literature, and modern languages, is strongly European in origin. Then too, there has been in recent decades a very explicit indebtedness of contemporary American philosophy to European predecessors. Of course, one should not underplay a rising scholarship in American art and literature and the strong development of indigenous philosophy.

History seems least to fit this pattern of looking toward Europe. History has a native tradition of scholarship, embracing at least a century or more of dignified independence from European models. It might be

argued that the social sciences and natural sciences are similarly indebted to European influences. But probably through the nature of
their subject matter, and their predictive rather than historical concerns,
they may claim greater independence. Further, the social and natural
sciences probably find themselves more at home in the technological
civilization of contemporary America, while the humanities, in some
respects, still move in the spirit of a preindustrial age. This proposition appears, therefore, to have some validity, more applicable to the
fields of literature and the arts and least applicable in the case of history.

2. *That the humanities are primarily concerned with values, the
sciences with facts.* This proposition is at once very popular and very
dubious. Its simplicity has enchanted many popular speakers on the
subject of sciences and the humanities, and a certain case may be made
for ethics and aesthetics with their attendant value concerns being
subsumed under one or more of the humanistic disciplines. But such an
argument overlooks the most important value of pursuing the "true"
and "correct," the province of all scholarship. At the same time it neg-
lects the meticulous concern of most humanists with the establishment of incontrovertible facts. Thus, the question involves more properly a different type of values pursued and a different order of facts
sought by the two classes of scholars. It would be an injustice to both to
assign them exclusive concern with either facts or values.

3. *That the humanities are primarily concerned with human experiences and actions.* The term *humanities* suggests that human reactions constitute a central focus, distinguishing such studies from other
areas of scholarship. It must be admitted that literary criticism, the interpretation of history, and the criticism of the arts confirm this
proposition. Still, this point of view may be overstated. History, for example, cannot ignore geographic and economic resources, nor can students of modern logic be said to concern themselves with mere human
subjectivities. Moreover, the social sciences such as anthropology, psychology, and even economics are surely and centrally concerned with
human reactions and experiences. So it seems to me that we are dealing here with a matter of emphasis. Indeed, many aspects of humanistic
scholarship seem quite removed from direct experience of human persons, though it must be granted that the humanities remain the primary
area of those intimate human concerns, the ethical and aesthetic.

4. *That the humanistic disciplines, in contrast with other fields, are
more deeply committed to the teaching function.* It is an easy thing to

prove statistically that humanistic scholars on the average are far more frequently engaged in teaching than most other types of scholars. It is also possible to prove that persons in the humanities declare their greater concern with the teaching function. Again, it is a common thing to find that the actual teaching loads of humanistic scholars in academic employment are higher than those elsewhere on the faculty. Finally, it is my clear impression that respect for the distinguished teacher, as opposed to researcher, is greater in the humanities. There is in fact a kind of tradition of the hero teacher, the arbiter of style and opinion, in the humanities, a tradition that has but a weak counterpart in other disciplines, notably the sciences, as scientists themselves frequently observe. This virtue of the humanistic scholar and teacher, however, may not be entirely self-elected, since humanistic scholarship is probably less divorced from the teaching function than most scientific research. But with this qualification it is probably valid to credit the humanistic fraternity with conspicuous dedication to the teaching function.

5. *That the humanities do not have agreed standards of proof and disproof but rather are dominated by the changing opinions of persuasive, individual scholars.* It is frequently said, mostly by nonhumanists. that the humanities have not accumulated a secure body of theory or doctrine. Rather it is their pattern to accumulate a growing body of subject matter whose evaluation is subject to constant and sometimes capricious reinterpretation as the standards of the times change or as eloquent and articulate spokesmen espouse new standards of judgment. The contrast to this pattern, so it is alleged, is contained in the pattern of modern science, which demonstrates a steady accumulation of theory and fact.

There may be some truth to this proposition, especially since the categories of taste and judgment are rarely invoked in the sciences but are deemed central to the most humanistic disciplines. Then too, the humanities have not the same devotion to a common "methodology" by which disputes may be resolved and "facts" established. But if the progress of humanistic scholarship seems less unidirectional and methodic than that of the sciences, there is still virtue to be found in this. It means that intellectual individuality among humanistic scholars is probably greater than among scientists. In fact, it is probably a requirement in the humanities that the scholar make a greater investment of sentiment and outlook than in the sciences.

6. *That there is a persistent distrust of quantification as a methodo-*

logical aid in humanistic scholarship. It is almost a commonplace to say that humanists have little instinct for mathematics and frequently abhor quantitative methods in the pursuit of their scholarship, deeming them both deceptive and pretentious when compared with their direct apprehension of their subject matter. Such attitudes have no doubt prevailed in certain humanistic circles, but it seems to me that they are rapidly giving way in the younger generation of humanistic scholars. Thus, modern philosophy is absorbed with many of the concepts of mathematics and quantification, textual criticism has recently availed itself of a variety of quantitative devices for the analysis of authorship and style, linguistics is everywhere employed with statistical techniques, while historians have long had recourse to economic, population, and other statistics. It seems to me, therefore, that the proposition is quite dubious. Its only validity lies in the probable fact that many humanists have little mathematical proficiency and that they have traditionally and necessarily trusted qualitative over quantitative evidence. The prospect is that humanists will increasingly employ quantitative methods.

7. *That the humanities have a subject matter in common, to which plural approaches drawn from other disciplines are applied.* It has been argued that the humanities have a fixed subject matter that is approached with a high order of electicism, while the sciences have a single methodology applied to plural phenomena. This hardly seems a valid generalization, though it may warrant some attention. It is probably true that scholarship in certain areas of the humanities may approach its subject matter from a very wide range of attitudes. History may be seen from an economic point of view, in terms of cultural currents, in terms of individual biography, in terms of aesthetic products, or in terms of the evolution of political forms. Again, as I have said, literary products may be evaluated in terms of textual characteristics, psychological motives of the author, or changing social and political forms. Thus, humanistic scholars may address themselves to their subject matter in the most catholic manner. This is partly true, however, of the sciences and social sciences, though in these instances there is a more inflexible commitment to objective proof and method than probably obtains in the humanities. This proposition, then, probably has some limited validity in affirming both the electicism and catholicism with which the humanist may address his subject.

8. *That the humanities, more than other disciplines, are necessarily immobile, being bound to a few distinguished library and museum collections.* It is, I think, statistically demonstrable that the humanities have not become so diffused as the sciences, social sciences, and technologies within the American system of education. That this is due to the necessary immobility of our great bibliographic and museum collections appears to me only a partial truth. The great museums and libraries of the eastern seaboard cannot readily be reproduced elsewhere and will probably continue to provide natural and preferred centers for humanistic scholarship. On the other hand, the greatly increased mobility of scholars, taken with modern methods of reproducing bibliographic materials, may sharply reduce the advantages that the East has historically enjoyed. Beyond this, the development of library facilities in many areas is moving with great rapidity while in the fine arts there is a second school of scholarship, emphasizing composition and performances, that bids well to be competitive with traditional art history. On balance, therefore, I am not disposed to believe that the immobility of resources will prove to be a major factor in impeding the diffusion of humanistic scholarship in America.

9. *That the humanities have been seriously disadvantaged in the intellectual arena by the strong and largely unilateral financial support of the sciences and technologies in recent times.* That the sciences and technologies have been abundantly supported financially both by the government and by industry is clear from any examination of the record. It is also clear that comparable support has not been given to the humanities, and this is a source of frequent complaint among humanists. There exists, for example, no major institute for humanistic studies at the present time, as Berelson points out. Moreover, the tradition of research contracts, governmental or private, is virtually unknown in the humanities. Humanists have indeed some right to a sense of neglect in the matter of financial support. The form that financial support might assume, however, is not altogether clear. Humanists are neither by tradition nor by temperament disposed to form the sort of corporate endeavors that characterize much scientific research. Neither are they commonly required to assemble costly apparatus. Probably the form that such subsidy should take is the endowment of individual scholars and their release from other activities, rather than the establishment of corporate enterprises or extensive physical facilities.

I think it may be fairly said that each of these propositions can claim some margin of support but that none can be unconditionally accepted in view of the variety and complexity of humanistic scholarship in America. I find myself, therefore, reverting to the assertion of the first chapter that the unity of these disciplines resides in part in their common historical origins, in part in the character of their subject matter, but primarily in certain qualities of scholarly attitude that I have designated as a special deference to style and sagacity. I doubt if any more explicit formulation can be effectively defended.

At the conclusion of this last chapter it is appropriate that I venture some tentative surmises concerning the future of the humanities in American civilization. Their present condition will perhaps bear brief restatement. As we have seen through many lines of evidence, the humanities, unlike the sciences and technologies, and certainly unlike professional and vocational education, have not claimed, generally, a powerful and incisive voice in higher education. Their effective recruitment and prosecution is, to a very great extent, in the hands of a select group of scholars heavily concentrated in eastern private colleges and universities. Only the more favored state universities, especially in the West, can claim comparable distinction. The Catholic system of higher education, while strongly committed to the humanities, has not yet attained the stature of these other two, and its future contributions cannot now be predicted.

Undeniably, social and intellectual forces are now abroad that extend the base of humanistic recruitment and scholarship. Our case studies of state universities have clearly attested to this. There appears to be a kind of cultural revolution in many schools that is raising the arts and the humanities to a new dignity and respect, and this augurs well both for the future of the humanities and for the redress of intellectual imbalances within our American civilization. But if left to natural circumstances, this trend may proceed but slowly. The main task, it seems to me, is to accelerate the infusion of humanistic thought and awareness throughout the broad fabric of American higher education. It is beyond the scope of this study to suggest the specific means by which this acceleration may be attained. But its realization would, I have no doubt, provide a sort of intellectual leaven that could lift our civilization to a new and truly creative epoch.

∽§§∾

APPENDIX: KEY TO ABBREVIATIONS
USED IN TABLES

Agnes Scott	Agnes Scott College
Alabama	University of Alabama
Albany	College for Teachers, Albany, New York
Amherst	Amherst College
Arizona	University of Arizona
Arkansas	University of Arkansas
Auburn	Alabama Polytechnic Institute
Augustana (Ill.)	Augustana College, Rock Island, Illinois
Augustana (S.D.)	Augustana College, Sioux Falls, South Dakota
Baker	Baker University
Barnard	Barnard College
Bates	Bates College
Baylor	Baylor University
Birmingham-Southern	Birmingham-Southern College
Boston C.	Boston College
Boston U.	Boston University
Bowdoin	Bowdoin College
Brigham Young	Brigham Young University
Brooklyn	Brooklyn College
Brown	Brown University
Bryn Mawr	Bryn Mawr College
Buffalo	University of Buffalo
California (Berkeley)	University of California, Berkeley
California (Santa Barbara)	University of California, Santa Barbara
Cal Tech	California Institute of Technology
Calvin	Calvin College
Carleton	Carleton College
Carnegie Tech	Carnegie Institute of Technology
Catholic U.	Catholic University of America
CCNY	City College, New York
Central Missouri	Central Missouri State College
Chicago	University of Chicago

167

Cincinnati	University of Cincinnati
Clark	Clark University
Colby	Colby College
Colgate	Colgate University
Colorado C.	Colorado College
Colorado U.	University of Colorado
Columbia	Columbia University
Connecticut	University of Connecticut
Cornell	Cornell University
Dartmouth	Dartmouth College
Davidson	Davidson College
Denver	University of Denver
DePauw	DePauw University
Dickinson	Dickinson College
Duke	Duke University
Emory	Emory University
Florida	University of Florida
Fordham	Fordham University
Franklin and Marshall	Franklin and Marshall College
Furman	Furman University
Georgetown	Georgetown University
George Washington	George Washington University
Georgia	University of Georgia
Gettysburg	Gettysburg College
Gonzaga	Gonzaga University
Goucher	Goucher College
Grinnell	Grinnell College
Hamilton	Hamilton College
Hampden-Sydney	Hampden-Sydney College
Harvard	Harvard University
Haverford	Haverford College
Hiram	Hiram College
Holy Cross	College of the Holy Cross
Hunter	Hunter College
Idaho	University of Idaho
Illinois	University of Illinois

Immaculate Heart	Immaculate Heart College
Indiana	Indiana University
Iowa U.	Iowa State University of Science and Technology
John Carroll	John Carroll University
Johns Hopkins	Johns Hopkins University
Kansas	University of Kansas
Kansas City	University of Kansas City
Kansas State	Kansas State University
Kentucky	University of Kentucky
Kenyon	Kenyon College
Knox	Knox College
Lafayette	Lafayette College
Louisville	University of Louisville
LSU	Louisiana State University and Agricultural & Mechanical College
Loyola	Loyola University, Chicago, Illinois
Maine	University of Maine
Manhattanville	Manhattanville College of the Sacred Heart
Marquette	Marquette University
Maryland	University of Maryland
Marymount	Marymount College, Salina, Kansas
Maryville	Maryville College
Massachusetts	University of Massachusetts
Miami	University of Miami
Miami (Ohio)	Miami University
Michigan	University of Michigan
Michigan State	Michigan State University
Middlebury	Middlebury College
Minnesota	University of Minnesota
Missouri	University of Missouri
MIT	Massachusetts Institute of Technology
Mount Holyoke	Mount Holyoke College
Mount Union	Mount Union College
Muhlenberg	Muhlenberg College
Murray State	Murray State College
Nebraska	University of Nebraska
Nebraska State	Nebraska State Teachers College

New Hampshire	University of New Hampshire
New Mexico	University of New Mexico
New Rochelle	College of New Rochelle
North Carolina	University of North Carolina
North Texas	North Texas State College
Northwestern	Northwestern University
Notre Dame	University of Notre Dame
NYU	New York University
Oberlin	Oberlin College
Occidental	Occidental College
Ohio	Ohio University
Ohio State	Ohio State University
Oklahoma	University of Oklahoma
Oklahoma State	Oklahoma State University
Oregon	University of Oregon
Oregon State	Oregon State University
Peabody	George Peabody College for Teachers
Penn State	Pennsylvania State University
Pennsylvania	University of Pennsylvania
Pittsburgh	University of Pittsburgh
Pomona	Pomona College
Princeton	Princeton University
Purdue	Purdue University
Queens	Queens College
Radcliffe	Radcliffe College
Randolph-Macon	Randolph-Macon College
Reed	Reed College
Richmond	University of Richmond
Rochester	University of Rochester
Rockford	Rockford College
Rockhurst	Rockhurst College
Rollins	Rollins College
Roosevelt	Roosevelt University
RPI	Rensselaer Polytechnic Institute
Rutgers	Rutgers, The State University

St. John's U.	St. John's University, Jamaica, New York
St. Joseph's (Brooklyn)	St. Joseph's College for Women, Brooklyn, New York
St. Louis	St. Louis University
St. Olaf	St. Olaf College
San Francisco C.	San Francisco College for Women
Sewanee	University of the South
Siena Heights	Siena Heights College
Smith	Smith College
SMU	Southern Methodist University
South Carolina	University of South Carolina
Southeast Missouri	Southeast Missouri State College
Southern Illinois	Southern Illinois University
Southwest Missouri	Southwest Missouri State College
Stanford	Stanford University
State C. of Iowa	State College of Iowa
State U. of Iowa	State University of Iowa
Swarthmore	Swarthmore College
Syracuse	Syracuse University
TCU	Texas Christian University
Temple	Temple University
Tennessee	University of Tennessee
Texas	University of Texas
Texas A & M	Agricultural and Mechanical College of Texas
Texas Tech	Texas Technological College
Trinity	Trinity College, Hartford, Connecticut
Tulane	Tulane University
Tulsa	University of Tulsa
UCLA	University of California at Los Angeles
Union	Union College and University
USC	University of Southern California
Utah	University of Utah
Utah State	Utah State University
Vanderbilt	Vanderbilt University
Vassar	Vassar College
Vermont	University of Vermont
Virginia	University of Virginia

Wabash	Wabash College
Wake Forest	Wake Forest College
Washington	University of Washington
Washington and Lee	Washington and Lee University
Washington State	Washington State University
Washington U.	Washington University, St. Louis, Missouri
Wayne State	Wayne State University
Wellesley	Wellesley College
Wesleyan	Wesleyan University
Western Reserve	Western Reserve University
West Virginia	West Virginia University
Wheaton (Ill.)	Wheaton College, Wheaton, Illinois
William and Mary	College of William and Mary
Williams	Williams College
Wilson	Wilson College
Wisconsin	University of Wisconsin
Wofford	Wofford University
Wooster	College of Wooster
Yale	Yale University
Yeshiva	Yeshiva University